Praise for
ALIEN AT HOME

"This body of work is amazing! The old saying holds true—'When life throws you lemons, make lemonade.' Get ready for an up and down rollercoaster of emotions in this journey of life-lessons.

"Here is a man who gets indoctrinated and seemingly hazed, at times, for doing what he feels is right. Sometimes we all find ourselves in familiar territory, but it feels so unfamiliar.

"Each character in this story is so true to life—particularly Fred, who is blunt, raw, and real. Sadly, racism is everywhere in this country. Dr. Joey Jumessi learns that the hard way.

"Great storytelling. The characters in this work are truly personified. Every new teacher and/or administrator should read this book. Within the content, are incredible motivational words of wisdom. There is so much happening under the surface (all) in the name of education. If you have achievable goals, then *ALIEN AT HOME* is a must read! So relatable for me. This book from the very beginning engaged and captured my attention. Author, Dr. A.F. Gnintedem, lays it out there while maintaining his dignity. What a great life-lesson!"

"Motivation is when your dreams put on work clothes."

> – **Stanley A. Bell, Ed.S.**
> Media Personality and Senior Communications Advisor
> Shelby County Schools

"Dr. Gnintedem's new book, *Alien at Home*, which centers around the life of an African immigrant in the American South, explores controversial topics such as xenophobia and racism with compassion and generosity. He resists the temptation to oversimplify human relationships with cliches and generalizations but instead, through his vast experience, guides the reader to explore the complexities of the immigrant experience. By describing the realities in Cameroon and juxtaposing them with the realities of the Southern Delta, a reader cannot help but be compelled towards compassion and insight and be challenged on a personal level as to each human's responsibility towards a better tomorrow."

> – **Christy Shriver, NBCT**
> Educator and Host of *How to Love Lit Podcast*

"An outstanding second offering from Dr. Antoine Gnintedem! As an educator who purveys Francophone culture, I assert that the point of view and experiences portrayed in *Alien At Home* provide a perspective that should be essential reading for my colleagues, in that it is imperative that French teachers do more than merely acknowledge francophone culture and narratives outside the Hexagon and Europe. Trepidation to include Francophonie arrives as lack of exposure and personal connections can stifle the urge to teach it, as to do so without expertise can feel insincere. Dr. Gnintedem provides a desperately needed lens by which American educators and laypeople may empathize with and appreciate the quest of immigrants who yearn for the opportunities available in the US, while showcasing a diverse and rich cultural mélange, exposing the humanity we all share."

> – **Teresa Floch**
> Immediate Past President, AATF TN;
> Technology Committee Co-Chair AATF
> Modern Languages Instructor, Rhodes College
> Teacher, Middle College High School

"A post-*bildungsroman* that explores the intersectionality of cross-continental racism in the United States. In prose of economy, the reader receives a stark vision of the present that gives way to a hopeful future, one filled with birth and rebirth."

> – **Jonathan May, Poet and Teacher**

ALIEN AT HOME

ANTOINE F. GNINTEDEM

atmosphere press

ALIEN AT HOME

FOREWORD

I'm drawn to stories that show a different perspective of the Sub-Saharan African immigrant experience. Stories that don't depict all of us as poor illiterate farmers and former child soldiers when we arrive in the US. Stories where the new arrivals are educated and intelligent, as opposed to the one-dimensional portrayals that occupy mainstream media. Like everyone else, I also want a story that entertains, educates, and is thought-provoking. ALIEN AT HOME is one of those stories. Antoine recounts that "other" immigrant experience with a masterful blend of fact and fiction that avid readers will love.

As a Nigerian-born, Cameroon-raised filmmaker based in Los Angeles, I actually feel like this book and Antoine's previous novel: *DOOM, GLOOM, AND THE PURSUIT OF THE SUN*, were written for me. They successfully capture that dual feeling of beauty and loneliness when you are caught between two cultures—simultaneously being both insider and outsider.

I had a conversation with him after we connected on social media, and two things stuck with me. One, he's a great guy. And two, he knows his stuff. What we are is usually different from how we're perceived. That means that the way we're perceived matters greatly, and I believe we should help our cause by looking for ways to change that perception. ALIEN AT HOME is leading that change. I hope you enjoy it as much as I did.

Tony Tambi Mbuagbaw
Writer and TV Star in @bobheartsabishola and @consequences_tv

PREFACE

As a result of my personal encounters with racism and xenophobia since I arrived in the United States as an exchange teacher in January 2004, I nourished the desire to write a book that focused specifically on the experiences of Black immigrants with these ills. However, for many years, I just couldn't find the time to dedicate to such a hectic undertaking because of my professional, family, and other personal commitments. Then in January of 2017, Donald Trump got sworn in as the 45th President of the United States and immediately went to work fulfilling the anti-immigrant policies that he promised his supporters during the 2016 presidential campaign, policies that legal experts, politicians, news media, national and international organizations, and most Americans polled all described as racist, nationalist, xenophobic, etc.

Thus, with the ascension of the Trump government to power, cases of violence against immigrants and Black people spiked nationwide thereby causing tremendous panic among the affected demographic groups. It seemed as if white supremacists and anti-immigrant groups viewed the election of the new president as a validation of the accelerated acts of hate that they were perpetrating with unprecedented boldness and viciousness. The equivocation of the President whenever he had the opportunity to condemn the acts of racism and xenophobia committed by his supporters further strengthened the perception that the spike in hate crimes was not unconnected to his election, and given the fact that he was going to be in power for at least four years, the anxiety among racial minorities intensified while the terror among Black immigrants like me became very palpable. Thus, I decided it was time to start working on the book that I always wanted to do.

In the spring of 2017, I collected data for *Alien at Home* and created an outline for the work, but when school resumed in the fall, personal and professional commitments again got in the way, and I was forced to table the project. Meanwhile, the violence against Black people and immigrants kept accelerating at a dizzying rate in America. Then, the heinous killing of George Floyd by a White police officer happened in May of 2020, and my distress and consternation, just like the shock of hundreds of millions of people who took to the streets in protest worldwide, spurred me to resume work on *Alien at Home*. At the time, I was quarantined at home due to the COVID-19 pandemic, and that allowed me the time that I needed to focus on the book and to finish it.

I hope you love reading and are inspired by this modest contribution to the fight to raise awareness about racism and xenophobia and to eradicate these evils from our beautiful planet.

Antoine F. Gnintedem, Ed.D., Ph.D.

To my wife, Shanda, for her tenacious love and her unwavering support of a prodigiously flawed being like me.

CONTENTS

Chapter 1: Go Back to Africa!   3

Chapter 2: The Outsider   12

Chapter 3: First Impressions   31

Chapter 4: New African Teacher   39

Chapter 5: Undeterred   56

Chapter 6: Not Alone   74

Chapter 7: Independence Day at the Goldmans'   97

Chapter 8: Growing in the Delta   119

Chapter 9: Going Home   128

Chapter 10: Milestones   172

Chapter 11: An Incredible First Week   189

Chapter 12: Heritage   195

Chapter 13: Derailment   204

Chapter 14: A Dove in the Tornado   212

CHAPTER ONE

GO BACK TO AFRICA!

"Go back to Africa!" the words written with a permanent marker on the rear wall of his classroom said. Instead of the shock and consternation that many people would feel in such circumstances, Dr. Joey Jumessi smiled. It was not the first time that racist and xenophobic statements had been made against him, and it certainly was not going to be the last. As a Cameroonian immigrant who had been teaching in the United States for over two years, hateful words like these had been hurled at him a million times by students, teachers, supervisors, parents, and total strangers when he was running errands around the city or just out for a meal or on a date.

For example, on his way to work earlier that week, he stopped at a gas station in Arlington, TN to do something that every car owner in the United does routinely: stop for fuel. While he was pumping the gas, a White male walked up to him and asked him for money to purchase breakfast. The man was carrying a tan camouflage backpack and had on blue jeans, a dingy white t-shirt, and Crocs. His face and neck were heavily tanned, and he looked like he could be in the mid to late forties.

"I'm sorry, I don't have any cash on me. I just have my credit card. Try someone else. Why don't you go into the store? Maybe they could give you something to eat," he told the stranger.

"I'm not asking them. I asked you, nigger! You can't even speak English. Why don't you go back to the jungle where you belong?" the beggar responded angrily.

Afraid of what the irate man could do to him, Dr. Jumessi quickly put up the pump, got into his car and sped out of the gas station, without even replacing the fuel tank cap on his Mercedes.

He stared at the distasteful words on the wall of his classroom, unfazed by the hatred of the hand that wrote them but wondering who wrote them and when. He pulled out his seating charts for all the six classes he taught daily and started reviewing them one by one. He easily identified all the students who were assigned the desk above which the hateful, xenophobic words were written.

He was not going to ask them; he was not going to do anything to them either. He was just going to keep his eyes and ears open during each period for any details that might reveal the identity of the budding xenophobe.

What troubled him the most about the situation was that someone could write on the wall of his classroom without his knowledge, because he was the type of teacher who was always circulating during each lesson in order to provide feedback, guidance and support to his students. In fact, in the four days since he started teaching at Bolton High School, he had been asked, at least twice, by his students, "Do you ever sit down, Dr. Jumessi?" They had noticed that he was constantly going up and down the columns and avoiding his desk that sat, neatly organized, in a corner of the classroom. He decided to put the matter of the slur to rest for that day because he needed to finish readying his classroom for meet-the-teacher conferences that were going to start in 15 minutes.

—

Bolton High school was one of over 66 high Schools in Shelby County School District. It was located in Arlington, TN, a mostly affluent and predominantly White part of Shelby County. With an enrollment of a little over 2000 students, more than 70% of the scholars were Caucasian, while the rest of the population was made up of minorities, including Black, Hispanic, Asian and Native American. On their part, the faculty, staff and administrators were not representative of the student demographics, as, of the more than 100 faculty and staff members, upwards of 95% of them were White, while the rest were in the above-mentioned minority demographic groups. The school was led by five seasoned administrators, including a White principal and four assistant principals among whom were three Whites and one Black.

Bolton had all the characteristics and perks of schools that were located in affluent, majority neighborhoods in cities around the United States. Unlike the previous school in rural Mississippi where Dr. Jumessi had taught, a school that was in a part of the United States that was overwhelmingly economically disadvantaged, Bolton High School had an impressively beautiful and vast campus that was more than the size of many universities in America.

The main building was the oldest part of the school, and it was inaugurated in 1887 on the site of the former Hoboken Plantation that was owned by Wade Bolton, owner of one of the largest slave trading businesses in the South and who, prior to his murder in 1869, set aside 1200 acres of land for the construction of an agricultural school. At the time of its opening, Bolton was operated as an agricultural and teacher's training college until 1911 when it transitioned to the Shelby County School System to become a high school in the district 14 years later.

Before his death, Mr. Bolton left an endowment for Bolton College which was passed on to Bolton High School, thus making it the only public high school in the State of Tennessee with a private endowment. When one added to the private endowment the fact that funding for predominantly or all White schools in the United States was on average ten times more than the funding for majority Black schools, one immediately realized that Bolton High was an incredibly financially capable school.

By 2000, many other huge facilities had been connected to the main building, which itself had been significantly remodeled, expanded and modernized. There was the two-story East Building, the two-floor North Building and the two-level South Building in addition to the two gyms, a cafeteria, a greenhouse, an ultra-modern auto mechanics shop and exterior sports facilities.

Both the interior and the exterior of the buildings were impressively clean, with crews sweeping, mopping and polishing the floors multiple times a day. The lawns were attractively manicured, while beautiful, bright flowers adorned the yard, walkways and lined the exterior of each building.

Apart from the tremendously amazing campus, Bolton also stood out from the rest of the schools in the State of Tennessee because of its rich course offerings. In addition to the standard courses available at most high schools, students at Bolton could take culinary arts, graphic design, nursing, cosmetology, criminal justice, auto mechanics, agriculture, Latin, German, and numerous Advanced Placement and International Baccalaureate courses, just to name these. Additionally, through a partnership with the University of Memphis, students in the 11th and 12th grades could accumulate dozens of college credit hours in courses like English composition, finite math, anatomy and physiology, philosophy, psychology, foreign languages, biology, English literature, speech, etc.

Similarly, the extracurricular opportunities available at the school reflected its affluent nature, as students at Bolton could participate in trap shooting, golfing, swimming, tennis, lacrosse, wrestling, bowling, knowledge bowl, debate, mock trial, swimming, and all sorts of activities that money could afford, in addition to the standard extracurricular domains found at most high schools around the nation.

On his first day at Bolton, right before first period started, a loud announcement came on the intercom, "The school store will be closing in five minutes! I repeat, the school store will be closing in five minutes. If you need any supplies, you better hurry before they close."

"I can go pick up anything you need for your classroom, Dr. Jumessi," a student offered.

"How far is the store?" he asked.

"It's right next door, in this same building."

"I need dry erase markers, manila folders and a stapler. I wonder how much they cost."

"Everything at the store is free for teachers," very loudly responded a fat, bearded, freckle-faced male in the back of the classroom.

Dr. Jumessi was going to tell him that he did not need to be that loud, but he quickly dropped it, amazed by what he had just learned about his new place of employment. He was teaching at a school that had a store where teachers could get anything that they wanted for instructional purposes free of charge. While at his previous job he had to buy basic necessities like paper, pencils, pens, staplers, rubber bands, tape, glue, chalk, etc., out of his pocket, at Bolton he could get any of these items, as often as needed, from the school without paying a dime. Additionally, school gear such as sweatshirts, shorts, t-shirts, sweaters etc. was free to faculty and staff, while students could get them and school supplies at deeply discounted prices.

"This is such an amazing school," he said as he got ready to start his first class on his first day at a first-class high school.

"Do you know that they have a food pantry here at Bolton too?" the young man in the back asked unnecessarily loudly again, derailing his teacher's plan for the morning. "It's loaded with all types for food, drinks, and snacks, and anybody can go there if they need food at home." As other students were about to confirm what their peer had just said, the teacher swiftly changed the subject to start his class on time.

He was happy he had made the decision to take the job at Bolton, an impressive high school.

—

It was therefore at this predominantly White and financially thriving institution that, Dr. Jumessi, a Black immigrant from Cameroon, had just found a distasteful racial slur imprinted on the back wall of his classroom just moments before parents started arriving for "Meet the Teacher Evening." As its name indicated, the event was the first opportunity for parents to meet their child's teacher in hopes of establishing a firm partnership that would result in their scholar's success that academic year. It was scheduled after the first few days of school so that teachers would have some preliminary, clinical feedback to give parents in order to inform some proactive decisions and strategies that the instructor and the parents could collaboratively implement to enhance the achievement of the learner.

There was a two-hour window, from 4:00 pm to 6:00 pm, set aside for the parent-teacher conferences, and parents had to make a reservation ahead of time to avoid more than the parents of one child from being in the room with the teacher at a time. Each meeting lasted five minutes at the end of which an announcement was made over the intercom for the parents to leave to meet the next teacher on their offspring's schedule.

Dr. Jumessi had just concluded his 11th meeting when a White couple arrived. They both looked like they were in their fifties. The husband was about 5 feet 10 inches, and probably weighed between 270 and 290 pounds. He had deep brown eyes, a thick, gray mustache and a goatee that contrasted sharply with his shiny bald head. From the black patches and spots on his blue button-down shirt which bore a name tag on the right breast and the even darker and bigger stains on his blue jeans and tan work boots, one could infer that he had just gotten off work at one of the numerous blue-collar businesses in Shelby County.

His wife, a blond with huge blue eyes, was about same height as he was, but she seemed to have been a lot more successful in watching her body mass index. She wore a white linen dress with lace design on the collar, around the edge of the short sleeves and all around the bottom edges that ended just above her knees. Her brown wedges added a few inches to her height and revealed her perfectly manicured feet and toes. The red polish on her toes matched her earrings, bracelets, and necklace. Even a blind person could tell that they were in the presence of a lady who cared a great deal about her appearance.

"Good evening, Dr. Jumessi? I'm Bob Flint, and this is my wife, Meredith. We're the parents of Justin Flint who's in your first period," the man said, shaking his son's teacher's hand firmly.

"It's a pleasure to meet you," Dr. Jumessi said warmly. "Justin is a brilliant and outspoken young man. He can be a little loud and talkative, but with proper redirecting and guidance, he gets back on task quickly."

"Yep, that's our Justin! He gets very talkative and playful to deflect attention whenever he finds any task to be challenging," the mother said.

"He has ADHD and is dyslexic," added Mr. Flint.

"I read about that in his IEP, and I have been...we, my co-teacher and I, have been providing him with all the accommodations and supports as prescribed by his IEP."

"That's so nice of you! Thank you so much for helping our son. So where does he sit?" Mrs. Flint asked.

"Over there, in the last desk in the second column from the other whiteboard."

Mr. and Mrs. Flint walked to their son's desk, and he sat in it while, while she looked at the elements of writing and other instructional posters that were on the wall.

Something caught her attention on the cinderblock wall, right above her husband's head. She froze instantly.

"Oh, my God!" she screamed painfully. Her face turned red, like all the blood in her body had converged in her facial veins.

Her husband sprang to his feet, and his eyes quickly caught what she was staring at in absolute consternation. He looked like he had seen a ghost, and his heart could be heard pounding very fast in his chest. It was obvious that both parents were incredibly offended by what was written on the wall above their son's desk, and their reaction made Dr. Jumessi suspect that they were not unfamiliar with the writer of the grossly insulting and racist words. They both turned around and looked at each other briefly, and, while fighting back tears, Justin's mother uttered, "We're so sorry, Dr. Jumessi! We raised our son better than this! We're not racist! We teach our children to be nice to everybody, to respect adults. We're not racist, Dr. Jumessi! Oh, my God; I can't believe this!"

"How did you know that he wrote that comment?" Dr. Jumessi asked.

"We know our son's handwriting. That's Justin's handwriting," Mr. Flint said emotionally.

The one-minute warning came on the intercom. Mrs. Flint took some tissue out of her Michael Kors purse and grabbed the container of dry erase board cleaner from Dr. Jumessi's co-teacher's desk and sprayed profusely and rapidly while rubbing frantically with the tissue, trying to efface the slur from the wall. Despite her efforts, the words stubbornly defied her. It seemed like the spraying and rubbing only made the letters frustratingly brighter. Her son had used a permanent marker, and, unless they were painted over, those words would be indelible forever. That was exactly what Dr. Jumessi wanted; he wanted the racist, xenophobic slur to remind Justin and anyone who espoused his views of their ignorance and hatefulness.

Even after the transition bell rang, Mr. and Mrs. Flint were still trying unsuccessfully to rub their son's words off the wall.

Before leaving, both parents apologized again on behalf of Justin, and they promised that he would be doing the same first thing in the morning.

The mea culpa from Justin did not happen, and Dr. Jumessi did not bring up the meeting with his parents or their disappointment.

Racial slurs had been hurled at him repeatedly by both Blacks and Whites since he started teaching in the United States. He had developed thick skin, and had accepted them as part of the Black, immigrant experience, although, on some occasions, mostly with adults, he would respond to the hateful words with particularly stinging sarcasm.

Furthermore, all through his life, even in his home country, Cameroon, belonging, being accepted by people, fitting in in communities where he lived, was often a problem. For instance, his entire family almost got lynched by an angry mob in the summer of 1990. The sea of blood-thirsty protesters, who marched to their home one hot summer afternoon and flung multiple Molotov cocktails at their modest dwelling, were fed up with the marginalization of Anglophone Cameroonians by the predominantly Francophone government, and, because Dr. Jumessi's family was one of a few Francophone families in Mbengwi at the time, they became an easy target.

Apart from the fact that they were not originally from that part of the country, the Jumessis were also targeted because Mr. Jumessi, the patriarch, worked for the national electricity corporation, a company that was viewed as one of the vehicles that the oppressive and corrupt government used to suck cash out of Anglophone regions, with little to nothing reinvested in the impoverished communities.

That traumatizing incident did not only scar him for life but it also significantly contributed to laying the first few layers of the thick skin that he progressively developed in the face of discrimination, hate, and rejection over the years.

CHAPTER TWO

THE OUTSIDER

With over 240 tribes (each with its own tribal language and culture) two official languages (English and French) and a transnational language (Pidgin English), Cameroon is both an immensely blessed cultural melting pot and an incredibly fertile ground for tribalism, xenophobia, and marginalization when governed by ineffective leaders who have no idea how to leverage the diversity and riches to enhance the nation's development.

About 80% of the country is French-speaking, while the other 20% speaks the other official language, and, since the reunification of Anglophone and Francophone Cameroon in 1961, problems started between the two linguistic communities due to the fact that the equality between both groups that was guaranteed in the constitution was not put into practice. For decades, French and Francophones consistently enjoyed special preference and elevation at all levels of national life to the detriment of English and Anglophones who were relegated to secondary status. While cities in the majority part of the nation flourished with better schools, roads, hospitals, businesses, and other infrastructure, the Anglophone regions saw very little development. To make things worse, Anglophone citizens needed to learn French to get services, do business and work in Cameroon, sometimes even in their own cities, towns and villages.

Because of the systemic marginalization of Anglophone

Cameroonians, radical citizens started clamoring for a secession of the region through groups like the All Anglophone Movement, the Cameroon Anglophone Movement, and the Southern Cameroon National Council. Militants of these organizations, especially members of the latter, frequently used violence to force the government to accept their demand for independence.

1990 saw an explosion of the anger and resentment that had been boiling due to these ills, in addition to the fact that there was a thirst nationwide for an end to the one-party system that had ruled the country since its independence in 1960. While some Anglophones wanted total secession from Cameroon to form their own country, others thought that the broader, national demand for a multi-party democracy would be a significant step in solving the problems that plagued the second of two English-French bilingual nations in the world.

As widely expected, the autocratic government of Paul Biya, who had been in power for 18 years, was neither in favor of the secession of Anglophone Cameroon nor was it welcoming of the idea of a multiparty, western-style democratic system of government. The vehement refusal of the president to allow such change sparked violence nationwide, especially in the English-speaking regions of the Northwest and the Southwest, and Francophones living in these parts as well as state-owned companies such as the National Water Corporation, the National Electricity Corporation, for which Joey Jumessi Sr. was the chief of center, the Cameroon Development Corporation, and many others, became very vulnerable targets of the rage of the desperate, frustrated, hopeless, and suffering Anglophone citizens.

Joey Jumessi Jr.'s family got caught in the middle of the combustible situation, because, as mentioned earlier, they were considered doubly "guilty." Even though his parents had been living in Mbengwi since 1963 and all of their children were born in the local health center, they were not spared.

Joey Sr. got the forces of law and order to secure his office and the company equipment and installations in the city, while his home and family were completely exposed to danger. The police and gendarmerie could only protect government property and the homes of the senior civil servants like the Senior Divisional Officer (SDO) and his assistants, the judge, the state counsel, and other top-ranking officials who, unsurprisingly, were all francophones. Because Joey Jumessi Sr. was just a simple head of the local office of the electricity company, he wasn't entitled to any protection. If he needed one, he would have to pay for it. He would have to get private security to protect his home and family, and that was impossible for two reasons: he couldn't afford it, and even if he could, everyone in the region that could perform such a job was Anglophone. It would have been like hiring the Taliban to protect the home and family of an American in Kandahar, Afghanistan.

One Saturday in June 1990, while the whole family was at the table having lunch, they heard an extremely loud noise emanating from the outdoor kitchen in the back of their four-bedroom house. Before they could even get up from their seats to go find out what had caused the bang, loud yelling, screaming and chanting came from the front of the house. Consequently, Joey Jr. went to check on the kitchen while the rest of the family, his six siblings and parents, headed to the source of the chanting to see what was going on.

What Joey Jr. saw in the corridor, between the main house and the kitchen, was gut-wrenching and tremendously scary to the 14-year-old. A Molotov cocktail had landed among several bags of corn on the cob that had just been harvested earlier that day and set everything ablaze. He quickly filled a bucket with water and emptied it on the rapidly spreading flames. It took twenty-four buckets of water to completely extinguish the fire, and by then, all the day's harvest, enough to feed the family for a year, was just a huge pile of charred black mess. He stared at it, panting furiously, shaking feverishly, absolutely confused.

While his dad had already warned him and his siblings that their family could be the target of angry citizens, he didn't think that they would be incandescent to the point of blowing up the homes of innocent citizens and dispatching them to their maker without hesitating.

"It must be some out-of-town people doing this," he told himself as he was frantically putting out the fire, because he didn't think that people he had known all his life and had referred to only as "Papa," "Mami," "Uncle," "Aunty," "Brother," and "Sister," depending on their age, would want to take out his family.

Meanwhile, on the opposite side of the house, a sea of seething strangers was the sight that awaited him when he was done drenching the flames. The crowd filled their yard and the neighbors'. There were people everywhere, as far as the eyes could see, covering the street, all the way to the main road. Some people had climbed to the top of trees and roofs because space was tight. Everyone came prepared to spill blood as each person carried whatever they could use for the purpose, including clubs, machetes, swords, spears, bows and arrow, knives, cudgels, pestles, engine blocks, tires, sticks, improvised explosive devices, and even hunting rifles.

While Joey Jr.'s four sisters and two brothers had concluded that they were about to be expeditiously delivered to their maker, and thus, were wailing and saying their last prayers on their knees, in front of the crowd, he joined his father who was pleading with the leader of the riot, a fellow that they both recognized easily due to his violent reputation in the city.

"You can't do this to me. I'm one of you. I've lived in Mbengwi amongst you and with you since 1963. Most of you in this crowd have not lived in this city as long as my wife and me," Joey Sr. hammered, mad as hell, although scared to his bones.

"You have every reason to be fed up with the way Anglophones in this country are being treated. You are right to be furious. I am too, because I have lived here long enough to be one of you, to feel what you're feeling. Even my own Francophone brothers and sisters don't trust me because they say that I am an Anglophone now, because I have lived here for 27 years now. My children were born here, and this is the only home they know. Mbengwi is our home! They attend school with your children; they play with your children; they eat with your children; they sleep in your houses all the time, and your children sleep in this house too; you are their family, our family! You can't attack your own family!" Joey's father added, with humiliating desperation.

Little Joey, as he was known in Mbengwi by many of the protesters, had never seen his father plead for anything. His dad, his hero, was the most proud, hard-working, courageous, protective, and smartest person he knew, and to see him in so much distress brought tears to his eyes.

"I wish I had one of the of those guns that fire endlessly in those Rambo movies. I would use it to make these people pay for rendering my father so despondent," the 14-year-old thought as tears flowed uncontrollably down his cheeks and drenched his white t-shirt that had "Mbengwi Rural Council" emblazoned on the front.

He took a step forward and stood right next to his dad, against his progenitor's wish, as he was putting himself in the crosshairs of whatever weapon was aimed at his most admirable role model. It was suicidal, he believed, but "...if an innocent child is going to be lynched by an angry mob, it would be honorable for him to die while taking up for his hero, his father," he told himself, as he stubbornly ignored his father gesturing for him to move back.

The leader of the insurrection, Mr. Fon, AKA Terror, did not budge. The tall, very muscular and thickly bearded Jack-of-all-trades tightened his grip on his machete, its blade glistening, ready to slice anything or anyone it was aimed at.

"We're tired of being marginalized and oppressed by the

government of La République," shouted Terror while brandishing his machete threateningly, dangerously close to Joey Sr.'s neck.

"All Francophones need to leave our land immediately!" he added angrily as he thrust the weapon toward the petrified homeowner's chest.

"This is the only home my children know. All of them were born here, and they have never spent a single day out of this town. Just because their parents were born in Francophone Cameroon does not make them any less Anglophone than you!" replied Joey's father angrily. He was done trying to reason with the rioters. Since it was starting to dawn on him that they were not going to spare him and his family, he became determined to spill his guts out.

"I know that no one here is interested in my plea for mercy and understanding, but, before you kill us, I want you to understand that we have considered ourselves at home here for the past 27 years, and we don't have anywhere else to go. Mbengwi is our home! My family and I speak Meta very fluently because we consider it our native language, and we practice the culture, our culture, with fidelity and pride, like you. So, you can kill us if it's going to afford you any comfort or happiness, but please know that you would be taking the lives of your own family," he concluded on his knees, tears streaming down his face as he submitted himself to be lynched first.

The last ditch rhetorical spill of the head of household and the lamentation and sobbing of his wife and children in the corner must have pulled significantly at the heartstrings of many in the crowd as they started dispersing, saying that they did not want to soil their hands with the blood of a family that, deep down in their hearts, they knew had roots in Mbengwi as deep as theirs or even deeper, as in the case of many of them who were neither born nor raised anywhere close to the town.

Similar traumatizing scenarios were playing out at the residences and businesses of countless other Francophone families and individuals as well as at government-owned companies in rural and urban areas in the Northwest and Southwest provinces. However, most of the terrifying visits did not have the same outcome as the one at the Jumessis, as many homes and businesses were burned to the ground, while their helpless owners sustained severe injuries, both physical and mental. State company buildings, cars, equipment and installations were looted and destroyed in Bamenda, Banso, Buea, Kumba, Mutengene, just to name these.

Meanwhile, upon learning about the plight of Francophones living in the Anglophone zones, sympathizers in the majority part of the country, especially in the Center, East, Littoral, South, and West provinces turned on Anglophone residents of their cities. This resulted in widespread, nationwide unrest with tremendous loss of life and property and a severe blow to the national economy. The impatient and brutal autocrat running the country unleashed the full force of the military, the gendarmerie and the police, who were notorious for their propensity for violence and abuse of human rights, to quell the uprising. An uneasy calm, enforced by the heavy presence of the armed forces, ensued in the country, especially in the Anglophone provinces after the tumultuous period.

Although the Jumessi family did not sustain any physical harm during the agonizing assault on their home, they, especially the children, were mentally and emotionally scarred forever. They relived the incident in harrowing nightmares night after night for many years. For months after the visit, Joey Jr. and his siblings did not want to venture out of the house due to fear and anxiety. His friends and classmates, with whom he spent on average 12 hours daily, attending classes, playing soccer, chasing girls, and doing other playful things teenagers in rural Cameroon indulged in, suddenly became untrustworthy to him.

That same day, as early as 9:00 am, he was playing soccer with seven of them before his mother called to say that he needed to accompany her and his siblings to the farm to harvest corn. In fact, three of his friends decided to join him on the trip, hoping they could gain a few more hours of play if they helped Joey finish his chore early.

Why didn't they warn him that his family was in danger, he wondered with profound disgust. He had made out the parents and brothers of some of his friends in the bloodthirsty crowd that marched to his family's compound, and he couldn't believe that his partners in crime were unaware of what was being plotted against every Francophone in the town, including the Jumessis.

The tormenting event also inflicted severe damage to the victims' trust of people that they had for decades assumed to be their fellow Anglophones, their fellow neighbors, their fellow tribesmen, their friends, and above all, their family. In the western world, particularly in the United States, the entire family would be an extremely urgent case for counseling and therapy for months, but in Cameroon, the rudimentary state of the healthcare system did not even have facilities, equipment and personnel to effectively handle physically ill patients, much less individuals with post-traumatic stress disorder (PTSD) and other mental and emotional conditions.

Therefore, like the thousands of other victims of the uprising, the Jumessi kids and their parents had to deal with the PTSD on their own and find a way to do so without being stigmatized, because, in Cameroon, any mentally or emotionally unstable person was just blanketly considered crazy and assumed to belong in a home for crazy people.

When Joey Jr. finally returned to school in the fall, a month after the first term had started, for the first time in his life, his teachers and peers started noticing that he had lost his trademark passion for learning, excitement about making new friends at the beginning of a school year, and his overall boisterousness. In the place of these, he was showing signs of low self-esteem and low self-confidence. He was frequently seriously disengaged and absentminded during class.

He urgently needed professional attention from a school psychologist or professional school counselor, but schools in the area did not have any such personnel. They dealt with students portraying his symptoms by whipping the crap out of them and suspending them with hard labor, including cutting the grass on the lawn using a machete, tilling the ground and planting crops in the school farm, cleaning classrooms, hallways, and bathrooms, and other forms of punishment that only aggravated the student's condition and further revealed the ignorance of school officials and the inability of the antiquated educational system to effectively address mental and emotional issues among students and staff.

Joey Jr.'s grades suffered significantly during the entire first semester, even in his favorite content area, English. However, his parents, who were usually unforgiving of any grades less than 100%, understood the impact of the mob's visit on their children, and they were willing to get them any help they could afford to get them back to where they were mentally prior to the heartrending incident. With the encouragement and coaching of his parents, siblings, and the parish priest, Joey Jr.'s grades improved rapidly and glowingly in the second semester, although the PTSD lingered.

Additionally, he got better at managing the symptoms of the post-traumatic stress as he got older. He would write in his journal, or go for a jog, or read a book, or watch TV, or talk to his parents and siblings whenever thoughts about the events of that fateful day suddenly emerged and threatened his emotional stability.

———

While the Jumessi children were not totally accepted as Anglophones in their hometown of Mbengwi, they were never fully claimed by the Francophones either. Since they were born, they had never been to the home of their ancestors, the birth-place of their parents, Foto, Dchang. Although Joey Sr. and his wife, Chantal Jumessi, were Francophones, and in spite of the fact that their last name identified them as natives of a tribe in the majority part of Cameroon, their children were neither considered nor treated as Francophones. Therefore, where the children were born, they were viewed as aliens, as physical representations of the autocratic, oppressive government run predominantly by self-serving and tremendously corrupt pol-iticians from the French-speaking provinces, while the linguis-tic and cultural group that the Anglophones considered the Jumessis to be a part of viewed and considered them as non-Francophones, as strangers or outsiders.

As a kid growing up, Joey Jr. never thought much about the implications of his unique linguistic and cultural back-ground. Whenever he did, he thought it was cool to be the only person in his entourage who was able to speak French. That occasionally gave him an edge in the competition for girls in the school yard. It also enabled him to make perfect grades effortlessly in the French class every time. It wasn't until that awful day when the angry protesters paid his family a visit that he quickly realized his predicament. How could his line-age, last name, and language skills be a liability, he wondered. The more he thought about the situation, the more depressed he became, and the more he wished he could be in a place where he and his family could be accepted for who they were.

Several years later, while he attended the University of Ya-ounde I, Joey Jr.'s feeling of otherness only got exacerbated by the persistent verbal and physical conflicts between Anglo-phone and Francophone students on- and off-campus. He rode all day with and was one thousand percent loyal to three friends that he had graduated high school with, but he also knew that they did not and would never trust him enough to count on him in any confrontations with individuals from the majority linguistic group, regardless of how hard he may have tried to prove the infallibility of his allegiance to them. Needless to say that his Francophone peers did not trust him either, not that he cared nor did he ever attempt to gain their friendship and confidence.

By the time he obtained his bachelor's degree in English and French (bilingual studies) in the summer of 1997, job and upward mobility opportunities were extremely scarce in Cameroon, and the few that were available overwhelmingly went to Francophones, whether they met the selection criteria or not. He applied for scores of jobs but received the same result each time: rejected. His friends were not lucky either, and, after a year of searching for jobs in Yaounde, any kind of work, they all decided to return home to their parents in Mbengwi.

For the next two years, just like hundreds of other jobless degree holders in town, Joey Jr. would idle around hopelessly. His daily routine consisted of reading, hanging out with other highly educated unemployed and despairing youth, watching television, and going to bed after dinner and starting over with little to no change in his schedule the next day. A little bit of comfort came from knowing that he was not alone in the predicament. In fact, if there were hundreds of unemployed youth with college degrees in a small town like Mbengwi, it meant that there were hundreds of thousands of them just in Anglophone Cameroon.

In August of 2000, one of his neighbors who was also his high school English literature teacher suggested to Joey Jr. that he should sit for the entrance examination into the training institution for secondary school teachers. It was a very long shot as the vast majority of the candidates who were typically admitted into the school annually either knew someone in the circle of power in the country or had deep pockets to bribe their way into the two-year training college, neither of which Joey had. After months of contemplation and weighing other options, he decided to give the assessment a try anyway, and, to his surprise, his name was on the list of successful candidates when the results came out a month later. His scores on the exam were so high that someone must have felt uncomfortable barring him from entering the training school based on merit.

Success in the exam meant that Joey had to return to Yaounde to attend the prestigious institution of higher learning, which was affiliated with the University of Yaounde I, his alma mater. While he was happy to be getting out of the desolation and despair that he, like most college graduates in Cameroon, had become accustomed to, he was not looking forward to attending classes with hundreds of Francophones who saw him as a second-class citizen, as an "anglofou" and several Anglophones who mistakenly viewed him as one of their Francophone enemies simply because of his first and last names.

Nevertheless, he applied himself daily and ignored the Anglophone vs Francophone drama that frequently unfolded on- and off-campus for two years. Some of these conflicts were often the result of the blatantly insulting treatment of Anglophone students by the almost-exclusively Francophone faculty and administrators of the school. As a testament to the monstrous nature of these individuals, they would teach and conduct official school business only in French and would compel the struggling Anglophone students to purchase their mediocre, subpar books and pamphlets if they wanted to pass their classes. This would provoke protest and complaints by the disgruntled students, but because of the complicity of the leaders, the acts of discontent would never gain any steam, and the students would abandon their quest prematurely, especially if the authorities used their favorite tactic: threaten to expel the protesters for violating the university's code of conduct.

However, through remarkable grit and grind, Joey Jumessi graduated from the Higher Teachers Training College with a master's degree in the teaching of English and French after two years. That guaranteed him a government job to teach in public secondary and high schools for life. It was not the career he dreamed for himself (he wanted to be a broadcast journalist), but it was a phenomenal bird in hand, one that would give him a bit of money to take care of himself and assist his parents and siblings. He could attempt to get into the school of journalism one day, but at least he would not be living off his parents or starving while waiting for that opportunity to come. And, if he was never admitted into the school because he did not meet the shady selection criteria, he would save money gradually or, perhaps, take out a loan to leave the country to study broadcast journalism in the United States or in England. His mind was racing with possibilities as he wrapped up his training at the teaching school.

Two months after graduating, the government released the assignments for his entire graduating class. He was assigned as French teacher to Government High School Nkambe, in Donga Mantung Division, in the Northwest Province.

The commune of Nkambe, which comprised of diverse villages, including Kungi, Konchep, Binshua, Bih, Saah, Wat, Nwangri, Mbaa, Kup, Chup, Bongom, Mbot, Tabenken, Njap, Binka, and Binjeng was about 20 miles away from the Nigerian boarder. Like Mbengwi where Joey was born, the citizens were predominantly Anglophones, and the only Francophones were government officials who had been posted there to serve in numerous administrative capacities. Even though he did not know anyone prior to his posting in Nkambe, he was glad to be going to a place that was not too different from his hometown. The proximity of the city to a continental economic powerhouse, Nigeria, also made him look forward to assuming duties in the city.

Unfortunately, he was paid barely enough for transportation from Yaounde to his place of work. Where was he supposed to stay? What was he supposed to eat? How about clothing, medication, and other necessities? How was he supposed to procure those without money? He learned upon arriving in the city that he was expected to live and work there daily while the government processed the paperwork for him to get a monthly salary, and based on past cases, the average time it took was 24-36 months.

Out of pity, his principal offered to let him live in an abandoned storage room on campus. The dusty, dilapidated and smelly, windowless 10×10 facility had no running water and no electricity. It had not been used in about a decade, and the dust and debris all over the floor was that old. With a flashlight and sunlight entering through a crack in one of the walls, Joey Jr. was able to look around the room, and it did not take him long to tell his boss, "Mr. Nfor, this is not going to work for me. I don't think you would even let an animal live in here. I'm going to return to Yaounde to figure out something. If I'm able to get a loan or some kind of assistance from somewhere, maybe I will come back, but it's impossible to live and work in such conditions even for one minute."

"If you leave, I'm going to tell the government that you've abandoned your job, and that means you would not get paid," the school administrator threatened.

"You do your job; do what you know is the right thing to do," Joey Jr. responded.

He left Nkambe in the evening. He stopped in Mbengwi for a week to check on his family and to seek his parents' advice. They offered him some money to return to his place of work, but it was not enough to rent a house and feed himself for up to a month. What would he do after that? Therefore, he decided to return to Yaounde to find a teaching job at a private school. Maybe he would have better luck with a graduate teaching degree.

The lord answered his ceaseless prayers, and he found a teaching job at Mevick Bilingual Grammar School two days after returning to the political capital of Cameroon. With money that his parents gave him, he rented a room in Bonamoussadi, a neighborhood inhabited primarily by university students, and every day, he would walk the nine-mile distance to and from work. In the excruciating heat that the city of seven hills was known for, that meant his days would be long and exhausting, but he had no other choice but to press on and hope for something better to come along eventually.

—

At a faculty meeting one day in early November, 2004, one of his colleagues asked him if he knew the previous French teacher who also hailed from Mbengwi, a guy named Austin Annenkeng.

"No, I don't know him, but the name sounds familiar. I think I have heard my parents talk about an Annenkeng family before. What happened to Austin? Did he resign?"

"No, he did not resign. He picked up a job in the United States through an exchange teacher program," the colleague responded.

"Oh, wow! That's amazing! I wish I could find something like that. Do you know the name of the program?" Joey asked.

"It was through an organization called Amity Institute. I checked it out because I wanted to apply, but unfortunately it's only for foreign language teachers like you," the colleague responded as Joey took out his notebook to write down information about the potential opportunity.

On his way home that day, he stopped at a cyber café at Carrefour Biyemassi to surf the internet. He searched the name Amity Institute and more details about the California-based organization came up, including their internship and exchange teacher programs as well as the selection criteria for each and the application process. Foreign language teachers with native or near-native fluency in the language were encouraged to apply.

Consequently, just like he did with the entrance examination into the teaching college a few years earlier, he decided to apply. He had nothing to lose, he told himself as he was frantically typing his responses to the multiple prompts before his time expired, because if it did, he did not have the money to purchase more credit to start the application over since it did not have a save-and-continue-later feature. He clicked on submit right as the timer on the screen was showing that he had two seconds left.

He continued teaching at the private school in Yaounde until February 2005 when the paperwork for his salary for the job in Nkambe was finally processed, and he received a lump sum after waiting for three years. Thus, he had enough money to help his parents and siblings and to use the rest to go and settle down in Nkambe, where the government had assigned him.

He had been teaching in Nkambe for three years when, at the end of March, 2008 the former principal at Mevick called to tell him that a large envelope had been delivered for him at the school, and he wanted to know what Joey wanted him to do with it.

"Where is it from?" Joey asked.

"It's from Amity Institute in the United States," the principal said

Joey's heart started pounding. "Please open the envelope and tell me what's in it," he instructed his former boss and waited impatiently for word on the contents of the envelope.

"Hello! Are you still there, Mr. Jumessi?"

"Yes, sir! I'm here. What's in the envelope?"

"It's a bunch of documents and a letter to take to the American Embassy to apply for a visa. It looks like you were selected for some exchange teacher program."

"Oh, my God! Oh, my God! Thank you, Lord! Thank you, Lord!" he could not contain his excitement.

He told the caller that he would be on his way to Yaounde the next day.

The application that he had casually submitted three years earlier had been deemed impressive by Amity Institute, and he had been invited to teach French at a high school in Indianola, Mississippi. When he read the letter that the director of the organization had written congratulating him on being among a few individuals selected out of more than 5000 applicants from around the world, he became very emotional. He saw the unique opportunity as a divine hand extracting him out of the precarious condition that teaching French in Nkambe was. In a part of Cameroon where there was unanimous abhorrence of anything Francophone due to the marginalization and oppression of Anglophones by the majority Francophone government, he was regarded as the enemy everywhere he went. To compare him to the representative of a detested colonizer would have been an understatement, and that made the job of teaching the colonizer's language to autochthonous people intensely miserable.

Consequently, he viewed his invitation to teach in the United States, the land of the free, as a golden opportunity to start a new life, a life of absolute freedom, one where he would not have to worry about the discriminatory and xenophobic labels and attacks he had endured his whole life. He would not have to wonder whether the people that he interacted with daily cared about him genuinely, or if they were just pretending and would twist his alien neck at the very first opportunity they had.

He had read voraciously in high school and college about the United States and had dreamed about the American ideals of democracy, equality, freedom and unity, and through an act of divine intervention, the opportunity to experience them had been given to him. It was the end of a seemingly endless period of being treated as a conditional citizen, like he did not fully belong anywhere in his home country, no matter how hard he tried to fit in.

Thus, when he departed from Cameroon on January 2nd, 2009, he was absolutely convinced, based on everything he had read in books, newspapers, and magazines and what he had seen in hundreds of Hollywood movies and documentaries, that he was going to a land where he would be accepted, where he would be free, where he would not have to watch his back all the time, a place where his self-confidence, self-esteem, and self-worth would not suffer persistent hits from individuals, institutions, and systems. "No more discrimination and marginalization, no more rejection," he said under his breath as his plane taxied on the runway at the Douala International Airport.

It was his first time being at an airport and seeing aircrafts other than on television, and the fact that he was actually traveling on one of the huge, beautiful, magically flying objects on that unique occasion was an exhilarating experience. Furthermore, since he did not know what to expect, everything about the flight made for a very special thrill, even the bumps, which at times were particularly rough and caused some passengers to scream with fear. During calm moments, while the plane glided smoothly through the clouds, Joey was the only passenger awake on board. The immense excitement he was experiencing kept him permanently stimulated all through the journey from Douala to his ultimate destination. Thus, while others on the aircraft were asleep, he watched movies and listened to music whenever it was too dark outside for him to stare at the clouds through the widow for hours. It was fascinating to see them up close, and he wished he could reach out and feel them with his hands, even for two seconds.

Once, as the bigger plane he was traveling on was sailing across the Atlantic, heading majestically to the United States, the bright sunshine that caused impressively beautiful sunrays, made everything outside so stunningly clear and pretty to Joey. He unbuckled his seatbelt in order to turn his body completely to face the window. His face had been glued to the glass for over two hours when he spotted another airplane about a mile or more away. It was flying in the opposite direction. The blue letters above the window spelled Delta. He wondered where it was coming from and where it was going. Was it transporting anyone or individuals who had left everything behind in their respective home countries and were in the pursuit of belonging and acceptance, what some called greener pastures, somewhere else? He thought about the possibilities that he hoped to find in the Land of the Free and the predicament of the people he had left behind, especially his loved ones, and it brought tears to his eyes. He dried his wet cheeks with his fingers and made a promise to God, there in the skies, as physically close to his lord as he would ever be, that as soon as he had the means and the opportunity to, he would bring his entire family to America to experience the life of peace, tranquility, and abundance that he believed awaited him in the home of Uncle Sam.

CHAPTER THREE

FIRST IMPRESSIONS

After traveling for two days, with layovers in Paris, France, Newark, NJ, and Memphis, TN, Joey finally made it to Indianola, a small city in the heart of the Mississippi Delta. Nestled between Greenwood and Greenville, MS, Indianola was a naturally beautiful place, with two major arteries, Highway 82, which ran through the city, linking it to the two bigger cities which sandwiched it, and Main Street, along which many businesses were located.

Unlike the American cities he had read about and seen in countless moving pictures back in his home country, Indianola was not a place with skyscrapers on both sides of streets and shiny limousines transporting gorgeous people who were clad in fancy clothes and adorned expensive jewelry. It certainly did not have any of the big factories, companies, and organizations that he thought were everywhere in America, nor did he see the round-the-clock hustling and bustling that he had anticipated finding. Indianola was a far cry from the fancy buildings, cars, places and people seen in *The Godfather* trilogy, *Coming to America*, *Rocky*, *Wall Street*, *Beverly Hills 90210*, *Friends*, *Matlock*, etc. Instead, there were farms everywhere in his new city, and many of the businesses were connected to the farming industry, such as seed supply stores, grain storage facilities, farm insurance agencies, farm loan services, pecan processing plants, catfish processing companies, tractor supply stores, farm equipment repair shops, etc.

On his first day out, Joey noticed that there were many dilapidated properties in the city, especially on one side of Highway 82, while on the other side, there were mostly bigger, beautiful, and newer pieces of architecture with expansive sodded lawns and colorful flowers. Some of the houses still had extravagant Christmas decorations hanging from the roof, trees, shrubs, windows and anything else that the homeowner wanted to embellish.

His host and tour guide, a White math teacher named Andrew, or Andy as he preferred to be called, took him down North Sunflower Avenue, then turned left on Second Street, in front of an old cotton gin, and right on BB King Road. Just a few feet from the start of BB King, they went across the railroad tracks, and Andy turned to his guest and said, "These railroad tracks cut across the city, separating South Gate from North Gate."

He added that South Gate was inhabited entirely by the Blacks, while all the Whites and a few African Americans with means lived on the other side of the railroad. Therefore, both the train tracks and Highway 82 pretty much did not only physically separate the two racial groups, but they also drew a line between the economically prosperous and the economically disadvantaged in Indianola, and Andy said that the same system was replicated in many other cities in Mississippi. He was not sure if it was done intentionally or unintentionally, but his money was on the former.

Andy was an average height, broad-shouldered, 160-pound, and athletic mathematician. He wore jeans and t-shirts with superheroes and famous mathematicians all the time, even to church. He complemented these with a pair of Jesus sandals or flipflops. A friend of his, Austin Annenkeng, also a Cameroonian, had linked him up with Joey after the latter reached out to his compatriot when he found out that the exchange teacher program had assigned him to the same school the fellow Cameroonian had taught at a few years earlier. Because Austin no longer lived in Indianola, Andy kindly accepted to welcome Joey into his house until he could find his own place.

A few hundred feet from the railroad, Andy and Joey arrived at Gentry High School where he was going to start teaching both English and French in a couple of days. The school, comprising mostly of outdoor-style facilities, was constructed in 1952. The driver parked the Toyota Yaris in the front parking lot and pointed at a brick building to his left, "That's the main office."

They alighted from the car and headed towards the gymnasium, a tan-looking building of the same material as the main office and the rest of the constructions on the campus. They turned left in front of the gym to get to the building housing the elective classrooms, one of which would be Joey's. Another left from there brought them to another long string of single-story classrooms for English, science, math, and computer labs. Directly in front of the long building and running parallel to it, was a facility housing the classrooms for content areas like JROTC and special education. The vice principal's office and the cafeteria were also in the same building. Across from the elective classrooms, separated by a driveway, was the vocational and technical center where students learned trades like auto mechanics and welding. Their last stop was the main building where the principal, counselors, and secretaries worked. There was also a copy and mail room there. The tour of the entire campus took about 15 minutes.

As they were touring the facilities, the exchange teacher was impressed by how clean everything was, compared to the schools he had attended or worked at in his home country. The classrooms had doors and huge glass windows unlike what he was used to. There were even freshly cleaned and frequently checked restrooms in every building, and some were reserved for faculty and staff only. Schools in Cameroon mostly had a few outdoor latrines that were hardly attended to, and every-one, from administrators to students, took turns using. There-fore, one could certainly imagine the joy that Joey felt about the restrooms at his new place of work.

As they were leaving the campus, Andy said that there were about 636 students enrolled at the school and that 96% of them were Black, while 3.7 % were White and the rest were Hispanic.

"If less than 4% of the students are White, where do all the White kids in this city attend high school?" Joey asked.

"They attend Indianola Academy, on the other side of 82. It's an expensive private school that, officially, welcomes chil-dren from all backgrounds, but, because the vast majority of the Blacks in this area cannot afford the tuition, 99% of the students there are White. IA gives scholarships to Blacks to at-tend, but whenever Black kids go there, they don't last up to a semester, because of the racist practices of the adults and stu-dents there."

On the ride back to the house that Andy and his room-mates were jointly renting on East Gresham Street, not far from Highway 82, on the majority Black side of the road, Joey was mostly silent. He had seen a lot that day, and most of what he had been shown ran contrary to the huge expectations that he had upon leaving Cameroon. For instance, although his readings did talk about racial discrimination in the United States, they left him with the impression that the bigotry was limited to human interactions or the lack thereof. Nothing pre-pared him for the blatant separation of a city into two distinct parts: one, mostly affluent, for the minority White citizens, and the other, tremendously impoverished, where the major-ity Black people lived.

At the dinner table that evening, Andy, who had noticed that Joey was not particularly thrilled about the tour of the city, probably made the decision to put everything bad about Indianola and the State of Mississippi, including racism and the abject poverty of mostly Black folks, on the table. Maybe he told himself, "If I tell him all the bad things about this city, he will appreciate the good ones even more whenever he comes across them." Thus, with his roommates, Joshua and Emily, they lectured Joey on the cotton plantations and cotton gins in the city where more than a century earlier, slave labor was used to make millionaires of many of the White families in the area. Physical remnants of the heinous practice were still standing in and around Indianola, and they promised to give him a tour of them soon.

Emily talked extensively about discrimination in the school system. She was particularly disgusted and troubled by the fact that the White community did everything to avoid any contact between the kids on the White side of 82 and the Black children on the other side.

"For instance, one would think that because there's only one school that Whites attend in the whole of Indianola, they would participate in athletic events and other extracurricular competitions with the predominantly Black schools in the city, but, hell would freeze completely before they would allow a sacrilege like that to happen." Indianola Academy preferred to travel for hours to "play ball" with schools of similar demographics in other cities and states.

Dinner was over at 7:30 pm, but they remained at the table until way past 1:00 am, chatting about the history of racism and the precarious state of race relations in 21st century Mississippi. The more he heard, the more Joey felt uncomfortable and almost regretful of the decision he had made to come to a place that seemed like what he had escaped from.

"If Black Americans could be treated with so much cruelty and discriminated against so intentionally and intensely, I wonder what kind of treatment would be given to a Black foreigner like me," he thought, frightened.

He had relied heavily on the glossy impressions of the United States that were portrayed in the movies, books, and other texts that he had read to inform his decision to move to the Mississippi Delta. He wished he had asked Austin about the city, the people, the culture, etc., but he was too excited to be leaving the deplorable conditions in Cameroon for "the land of the free" that the only thing he asked his compatriot was help with a place to stay until he could find his.

He rested a few hours that Sunday night, and the next day, Emily took off work to drive him to the Social Security Administration office in Greenville, MS, so that he could apply for a social security card. Her tremendous kindness was heartwarming, and Joey let her know how immensely grateful he was.

She was an impressively attractive, fit, guitar-shaped brunette. She stood about 5'10 with long, straight, and shiny hair that looked freshly done all the time. Her skin, at least what was visible, was so smooth and looked like that of the rich White ladies he had seen in magazines, movies and TV shows. It was obvious that she took meticulous care of herself. Joey noticed that she did not wear any makeup. She did not need any, as phenomenally pretty as she was.

Her body-hugging jogging outfit revealed such mesmerizing features that would make a saint sin in his thoughts. The 24-year-old from Bear, Delaware, was also incredibly informed and curious.

She had joined Teach for America a year earlier to educate children in an economically disadvantaged community. The only child of parents who were both very successful accountants, Emily could have chosen to do something else with her life after college, something more financially rewarding in the state where she was born or in a bustling metropolis close to home, such as Washington, DC, New York City, and Philadelphia, PA, but she preferred to teach Black kids in Indianola because she wanted to make a difference. More concretely, the systemic racism that was particularly obvious in the Delta was too hard to ignore. Teaching Biology at Gentry and educating people, especially White Americans about racial equality, racial equity in educational opportunities, and racial diversity was, in her opinion, a way to contribute to a solution to the evil. All her attributes made her strongly likable, and Joey found himself developing interest in her.

After driving for 28 minutes and chatting the entire time, they made it to the social security office. He was second in line, and it did not take long to fill out the paperwork. Thus, they were out of there within minutes.

Before getting back on Highway 82 to return to Indianola, Emily decided to give her passenger a quick tour of Greenville. Joey quickly noticed that the city was more developed as it had better streets, taller buildings, more businesses, and a bigger hospital. It even had a regional airport and a river port with a massive floating casino. After the rapid tour, they headed home.

As she was driving, Emily continued asking questions about Joey's family, where he grew up, where he attended elementary school, middle school, high school, and college, and, oddly, if he had a girlfriend. She also inquired about politics, economy, culture, religion, sports, and inter- and intra-community relationships in Cameroon. Her guest made sure to provide the most accurate and objective responses to all the questions, and they just made her want to know more. She told him that she had been nourishing the desire to visit Africa since when she was in high school, and that Cameroon sounded like an interesting place to start because of all its diversity, complexities, and riches. They stopped at the McDonald's in front of the Sunflower Food Store in Indianola to pick up lunch before continuing home.

While Emily spent the rest of the day preparing for the next day of school, Joey stayed in his room, reflecting about everything he had learned thus far about the Mississippi Delta. Although most of what he had seen and heard did not align with the readings, movies, and dreams that had lured him to the United States, he concluded that he would spend more time researching and learning more about the incredibly complicated country. "Things may just not be as bad as they seem," he thought. He was going to find out.

CHAPTER FOUR

NEW AFRICAN TEACHER

On his first day of school, Joey rode with Andy who volunteered to help him get his classroom together before students arrived. Joey was the first certified, full-time teacher that the students would have since the school year started in the fall of 2008. Multiple substitute teachers had been in and out of the classroom until his arrival, and anyone who has worked in education knows that kids, especially teenagers, without a steady teacher are just like animals that have roamed, unsupervised for a long time, and it takes a high dose of consistency, firmness, patience, rigor, structure, and understanding on the part of anyone who desires to get them back on a productive path. Could a teacher from a foreign country with a totally different culture and education be up to the task?

Joey's classroom was in the electives building since he had four sections of French and two of English. The room was tidy, with desks neatly lined up in six columns of five on shiny blue and white vinyl tiles. Anticipating that he would not have time to set up his classroom before his first day of school, the principal had instructed the plant manager and the head of the English department to get the room ready as best they could, and the exchange teacher would give it his personal touch upon his arrival. The white walls of the room were bare, and there were English and French textbooks as well as reference resources stacked up below a long, green chalkboard in front of the classroom. About two feet from the right edge of the board was an old, metallic desk that wobbled when Joey placed his black leather briefcase containing books on it. There was a low chair behind the desk with its back against the wall. The last person to sit in it must have been very vertically challenged, he thought.

To create more space in front of the classroom, Andy helped Joey move the desk to the corner, farther from the board, but closer to the only other wall that had windows, three of which were permanently shut. The desk was strategically placed thus so that, if he were to sit down during class, he would be able to have his eyes on the board and on his students.

"It's almost time for first period. The students will start arriving in 10 minutes. Do you need help with anything else before I go get ready for my class?" Andy asked.

"No, you have done a lot already. Thank you so much for your kindness and generosity," Joey responded, picking up a piece of white chalk to write the day's objectives for his French and English classes on the board.

"Have a wonderful first day of school then, and remember, I'm just one building away if you need me."

"Thanks, Andy! You have a great day too," the guest said with energy and excitement.

First period was disappointedly shocking; it was dizzyingly devoid of the incredibly informed and knowledgeable learners he was expecting to find in 21st century America, the age of information at the fingertips of everyone, even in rural parts of Africa. Most of the 55-minute class was spent going over classroom expectations and procedures and answering questions that the students had, including many about Joey's family, the educational system in Cameroon, the types of religions Cameroonians and Africans practiced, the weather in his home country, etc. Many of the things that the teenagers were particularly curious about revealed that they thought that the continent of Africa was inhabited by barefooted, filthy, ignorant, naked, uncivilized, herbivorous and carnivorous humans who subsisted by farming, fishing, and hunting all day, using rudimentary, traditionally made tools like hoes, spears, bows and arrows, cudgels, machetes and knives. Similarly, his students believed that Africa was a primitive continent where the people lived in tiny mud huts and on trees in the jungle, like monkeys.

The level of ignorance revealed in that first period class made Joey wonder if the students were genuinely unknowledgeable about the continent on which civilization began, or if they were just implicitly insulting him while wasting time. He would soon discover that his students, just like many adults on- and off-campus, had very insane misconceptions about Africa and Africans which resulted in them saying things that were extremely disrespectful and insulting to and about anyone from the continent, whether intentionally or unintentionally.

By the end of First period, word had spread on campus that there was an elegantly dressed, fit, handsome, bald, multilingual, and very sophisticated African teacher on campus. Some students thought that Mr. Austin Anenkeng had returned when they heard this and quickly rushed to the foreign language block of the school. Everyone wanted to see who that foreign teacher was, thus the traffic in the hallway was unprecedently high during transition to second period. The latter class and the one immediately after were not dissimilar to Joey's maiden appearance in front of American high school students.

He went over expectations and procedures, but the kids were more interested in confirming what they knew about Africa. Many of them did not believe the answers he gave to their questions. For instance, nothing he said could convince some that he brought all the nice threads and shoes he wore from Cameroon. He projected pictures and videos of buildings, cars, people, and schools in Yaounde, Pretoria, Lagos, Accra, Abidjan, and Libreville, but many of them chose to hold on to their beliefs about Africa, leaving Joey wondering where they got those disturbing ideas from and why Black Americans would be so blatantly ignorant of the continent from which their ancestors were violently stolen.

As his first day progressed, his students' questions got more and more ridiculous and outright discourteous. Some of them started making smacking, hooting, grunting, panting, growling, and cooing vocalizations and shouting "Awawa," "Buyaka Buyaka Buyaka," "African Booty Scratcher," and a few other slurs whenever he turned to write something on the board. Whatever the reaction the handful of impudent and unmannerly students hoped to get from him, he clearly disappointed them by staying calm and ignoring the teenage display of shameless impertinence.

He was angry and frustrated, but he told himself that he needed to stay cool, collected, and confident and not let a group of uncivilized teenagers make him lose it. "Maybe they are just trying to see if they could run me off so that they could continue to have the free time and freedom that they have been having since the school year started," Joey wondered. He was not going to grant them that wish, if that was what they wanted.

While debriefing with his housemates later that day, they gave him insightful classroom management ideas such as assigned seating with strategic seating charts, progressive discipline steps that included verbal warning, conference with student, phone call home, teacher-assigned detention, parent conference, and, if all of these failed, referring the students to the administration for appropriate disciplinary measures such as in-school suspension, out-of-school suspension, and even expulsion, depending on the gravity of the offense. Andy, Emily, and Joshua emphasized positive behavior reinforcement to address the issues that Joey faced that day. They encouraged him to recognize and reward the students, however few, who upheld the classroom expectations and procedures.

Seeing their peers getting praised and rewarded could make some or all of their ungracious peers envious of them and desirous of similar privileges. It was a kind of reverse psychology that they urged their new friend to try.

Implementing the strategies dramatically improved the learning environment and allowed for some highly productive class periods. The only impediment to the level of productivity that he aspired was the acute shortage of instructional resources at Gentry High. He was an avid proponent of project-based learning which involved a high degree of collaborative tasks requiring the use of computers for research, data collection, analysis and evaluation of data, discussion of findings, and multimodal presentations. Access to current, comprehensive, and credible sources like books, journals, and magazines was also crucial to the effectiveness of that approach to teaching and learning. Because of the dire economic situation of the schools and families on the side of the train tracks that Joey's school was located, it was incredibly challenging for him to accomplish many of the things that he desired for his students.

Consequently, he and the kids did the best that they could with the terribly limited means that they had to make teaching and learning impactful, meaningful, relatable, and successful every day. If he needed to use the computer lab, the only room on campus with enough computers for everyone in any of his classes, he had to reserve it two weeks ahead of time, to give the computer applications teacher, whose classes met in the room daily, ample time to make other arrangements for her students, perhaps relocating to the library, which had a few workstations, although the librarian required several days' notice from anyone who needed to use it for class.

Similarly, whenever he needed to make photocopies of readings, graphic organizers, worksheets, and other texts needed for his classes, he had to submit the original document to the secretary in the main office a day in advance with information about the type and number of copies needed. He hated going to the main office for that, not just because of the delay it caused in getting copies on time, especially when multiple teachers were submitting requests for copies at the same time, but mostly because the secretary treated him disrespectfully by using hateful and insulting language in addressing him on his first day at the school.

In fact, Ms. Washington, a thirty-something-year old African American who had never ventured out of the Delta since she was born, let Joey know that he was not welcome at Gentry and in the City of Indianola because immigrants like him were "...coming over here and taking our jobs from us, making it hard for us to find work to feed our families."

Andy, Josh, and Emily were livid when their guest revealed to them what the secretary said to him when he went to the office on his first day at the request of the principal, and they insisted that he report her to the school leader, something that he chose not to do, out of fear of retaliation. He was brand new at the school and in the country to venture into something like that without knowing who was who and how people reacted to complaints and reports about them. Also, he thought about a slogan that he had heard several times in the American movies and documentaries that he had seen back home in Cameroon: "Snitches get stiches," and he was certain that he did not want anything like that happening to him 17,000 miles away from his loved ones. Thus, he made do without copies as much as he could, and whenever he absolutely needed to have some made, his housemates, who had been his fierce supporters since day one, would take turns submitting the required requests on his behalf.

Meanwhile, during his first weeks at Gentry, Joey and Emily spent a lot of time together after school. She helped him with instructional planning, finding and creating assessments and teaching materials using the computer and the internet, two modern technologies that he did not yet master as much as she did. Additionally, more often than the other roommates, she drove him whenever he had errands to run, and she would let him drive her car with her guidance from time to time as he had never driven a car prior to moving to the United States. The more time they spent together, the closer they got to each other, and one Saturday, after having dinner at a Greenville restaurant, they drove to the park down from Greenville Weston High School to walk the trail.

After 30 minutes of meandering around the park, they were exhausted and decided to sit down at one of the open benches. They were silent for over five minutes, mostly catching their breath and admiring the beauty of the plants and trees around them, then, suddenly she turned and looked at him like she expected him to say something. As much time as they had been spending together lately, he had never really looked into her eyes intentionally, but that evening, he could not keep his away from hers as she stared at him mesmerizingly.

Her shiny blue eyes were particularly remarkable as the sun was setting, gradually making way for darkness to cover the river city. He was about to tell her how impressively beautiful and gorgeous she was when she slid closer to him on the bench, causing him to lose his train of thought. What was unraveling right in front of him was surreal, and he wondered if he was not dreaming. It was true that he found her very attractive and well within his reach whenever he wanted to make a move on her, but he just did not imagine it being so soon and, especially, he did not imagine a situation where he would not be the one making the first move. Thus, he put his right hand across her shoulder, and she almost instantly rested her head on his shoulder and lowered it down to his chest. Her long, silky, straight hair smelled like fresh spring roses that close. Whatever was happening, he did not believe it, but he did not want it to end either. They maintained that posture quietly for about six minutes, then she looked up and asked gently, "Are you okay?" He nodded in affirmation, then, without warning or anything, their lips locked as they kissed passionately, like two love-starved individuals for over three minutes, until Joey remembered where they were and suggested that they head home to Indianola. Thus started an intensely romantic relationship between two people who had secretly admired each other for over nine weeks.

Joey's social security card arrived in the mail the following week, and he was very excited until he opened the envelope. His card was very similar to Emily's and others that he had seen except for one thing: written across the top were the words, "Valid for Work Only with INS Authorization." Therefore, his very first piece of identification in the United States labeled him as a foreigner. A series of other events happened during that period to remind him that, while he was allowed to form the minds of future American leaders, doctors, lawyers, bankers, educators, accountants, engineers, pilots, politicians, and other professionals, he still was an outsider with limited rights and privileges.

On the day that school dismissed for spring break, he had an appointment at the Department of Motor Vehicles in Greenville to get his driver license. Because he had been practicing driving with Emily, Andy, and Josh, he very easily passed the test to become an authorized Mississippi driver. However, the joy of the moment was quickly soured when an agent called him to the counter to collect the important piece of identification. As soon as it was handed to him, he immediately noticed the "otherizing" phrase that cut across the document: "Non-US Citizen Driver License." Those words, along with the above-mentioned ones on the social security card were an albatross around his neck from then on, complicating minor and major steps in life that were fluid to the average American. They rendered exceptionally difficult, almost impossible for Joey things that Black Americans typically faced overwhelming challenges getting due to the systemic racism prevalent in the country.

For instance, with valid identification and a clean record, opening a bank account is often a walk in the park, especially for someone with a career, but it was not the case for Joey. When he tried to open one at the Planters Bank on Catchings Avenue in Indianola, he was told that it would take a while because special approval had to be obtained from senior management before an account could be opened for someone with his type of papers. Regular US citizens had their accounts opened within minutes, but he was made to sit in a waiting area for several hours until one of the vice presidents, an old White gentleman, finally showed up and took him to a corner office where he was interrogated about where he was from, why he was in the United States, for how long, why he needed an account, what he did for a living, and other ridiculous questions. Although his wish was eventually granted, it happened after hours of uncomfortable, humiliating, and dehumanizing grilling that made him feel like he was being suspected of money laundering, terrorism, illegally funneling money out of the United States, and other criminal enterprise. Halfway through the questioning, he felt like telling the banker, "I don't understand what you are insinuating with all these questions, but I will not be needing a bank account anymore, at least not one with this bank," but he concluded that walking away would only lend credence to whatever the White gentleman was insinuating, and he was not going to let him or anyone else have the wrong impression about him.

With that speed bump surmounted, he turned to another vital need, a car. His housemates so generously and gracefully gave him rides to anywhere he wanted to go and refused to take his contribution for gas, but something his father always told him and his siblings would not let him continue to depend on them for transportation as soon as he had enough money to get his own car. According to his dad, "If you can avoid depending on people, always take that route, because you would be respected more if you're independent." He heard these words re-echo in his mind over and over each time he was offered a ride to work or to run errands and each day that he benefitted from total strangers' benevolence for a place to stay.

Thus, because of the testimonies of owners and the reviews he read about the reliability of the Nissan Maxima, he attempted to buy one, but he was turned down for financing everywhere he went. At two dealerships in Greenville, he was told that, although he made enough money to very easily afford the monthly car note on the type of car that he wanted, he could not be approved for the loan. The official reason given was that, due to his recent arrival in the United States, he did not have any credit history.

However, Emily, who had accompanied him to the dealerships called out the ridiculousness of the reason for rejection, as she said that she knew of at least two very close family friends who were easily approved for car loans weeks after immigrating to the United States from Germany through the Diversity Visa Lottery Program. In fact, one of them did not have any complications getting a mortgage either just six weeks after arriving in Delaware. Although both individuals did not have any credit history, they did possess something very credit-boosting and credit-worthy that Joey would never have: they were White. One of them, a lady, worked as a waitress at a restaurant at the time of her loan approval, while the other, a male, worked with a landscaping contractor who was also a German immigrant.

It was difficult to prove that Joey was turned down because of his race, but, given the fact that he had a great, reliable, and stable job with a good salary, no other bills, and no dependents, and given the fact that he could pay a significant down payment and still afford to double the monthly car note, it seemed very unlikely that his race and immigrant status, which was highlighted on his newly-obtained identification documents, were not factors in his disqualification.

He was stunned to notice that what he had read in a *New York Times* article about the discrimination against Blacks in loan approval processes around the United States was happening to him. The article that he had read mentioned the fact that Black borrowers with similar profiles as White loan applicants were treated differently by financial institutions around the country on the basis of their race. While the White borrowers were very easily granted low interest loans with very little paperwork, Blacks and Latinos were required to submit tons of documentation only to be turned down for the loan or approved at extremely high interest rates.

A colleague advised him to try another dealership in Greenwood as he believed that Joey would have better chances of getting a car loan approved there. Unfortunately, the outcome at Wilson and Wilson Car Center was not particularly dissimilar to the other places Joey had already been. He was told that he would have to buy the Nissan outright, because, according to the general manager, Mr. Ashton Wilson, immigrants were widely known for buying cars on credit in the United States and disappearing with them to other countries. The fact that the loan applicant was a teacher in a neighboring city did not make any difference.

As a last resort, Josh, his housemate suggested trying a used car dealer on Highway 82 in Leland, MS. After test-driving a silver, 10-year-old Nissan Maxima that was still in amazing condition, Joey sat down in a small, mobile home office to fill out another loan application. He handed it to the owner of the business when he was done and waited anxiously. The car salesman, a tall, skinny White guy in his sixties, entered Joey's information into a computer and asked to see his driver license. A copy of the identification was made and, a few minutes later, Joey was told that his loan was approved at 17.99% APR. They went over the terms, and he reluctantly initialed and signed the marked sections. With taxes and everything, the car cost $16,964.00. He paid down $5,000.00 and would pay $300.00 monthly until the loan was paid off.

He drove back to Indianola in a car, not the new Nissan Maxima that he wanted, but in a much older model. As a result of the usurer-type interest rate, the achievement was not one he thought was worth celebrating. However, it was impossible to place a monetary value to the independence that owning a car afforded him. No more relying on friends and well-wishers to offer him rides to work and to errands in and around the Delta. Freedom was priceless. To a man, especially an African man, nothing was less manly and more manliness-degrading than having to depend on a female that he was romantically entangled with for his mobility. It robbed him of the self-confidence and self-pride that women loved to see in any suitor that was deserving of their attention and love. As much as he was happy and thankful for his friends' generosity toward him since his arrival in the United States, he was incredibly eager to start flying with his own wings, and getting his own means of transportation was the first wing.

The day after he bought his "new" car, he excitedly showed it to Major Brown, a retired Special Forces soldier and ROTC instructor at Gentry. The light-skinned, very tall, slender, and very athletic, baldheaded, retired US Marine with a haystack-thick moustache had taken a special interest in Joey since his arrival and loved to talk to him about his missions to African countries like Kenya, Tanzania, South Africa, Nigeria, Ghana, Senegal, Libya, Tunisia, Ethiopia, Somalia, and Egypt when he was in active duty. "For a poor Black kid from the MS Delta, apart from the pride of serving my country around the world, I was particularly happy about the opportunity to discover the continent from which my ancestors were kidnapped and brought to the United States close to 400 years ago," the Afrocentric sexagenarian said, teary-eyed, the first time they spoke, a couple of weeks after Joey's arrival in Indianola, right before a faculty meeting.

"The Nissan Maxima is quite old, but it will take me

around, and that's more important than anything else to me at this time," said Joey as he tossed the keys to the Marine who asked to take the acquisition for a test-drive in the parking lot behind the computer lab. The recent car owner recounted to Major Brown all the hurdles he had to overcome just to get a car loan at a cutthroat interest rate, even though he had a significantly better income than most people in the Delta. "Welcome to America!" the veteran soldier interrupted him. "That is what Black people endure in this country on a daily basis." As he was slowly snaking his way among parked cars in the parking lot, Major Brown gave his passenger a personal account of racism. He talked about his grandfather being followed home one night in 1962 and killed in front of his wife and children by three White men because he had passed them on a dirt road in his Chevy C10 pickup truck. They forced his family to watch as they tortured him to death. "Years later, my uncle stopped to buy cigarettes at a gas station in a small town outside Jackson, MS on his way to the coast, and when he came out of the store, a group of teenage White boys accosted him and started taunting and beating him up with bats, brass knuckles and belts. The sad thing is that other White people saw what the boys were doing to him but did not even raise a finger to help him. When they were done beating, kicking, and punching him, they tied his legs to the back of their pickup truck using barbwire and dragged him along a country road for miles until he gave up the ghost. They eventually dumped his disfigured body in the woods."

"Did the people who killed your grandfather and uncle get the death penalty for their heinous crimes?" Joey asked, disgusted by what he had just heard.

"They were never arrested, even though everybody knew who they were," Major Brown responded, fighting back tears. "That's America, a nation of two realities: one for the White people and one for the Blacks and other minorities," he added. He went further with a story about how he was passed up for promotion eight times in the military in favor of White colleagues with far less experience and education. "There were also the countless occasions when, as the lone Black member of my team, my colleagues would totally ignore me during strategy meetings and act as if I was not even present." Furthermore, he mentioned the time when he eventually made the rank of captain although all the White colleagues in his cohort were at least majors. "I was very happy nonetheless, until I started having all kinds of trouble with those under my command and those above me. The former refused to take orders from a Black leader, while the latter would ignore my ideas and suggestions, but would turn around and do exactly what I had suggested and would take full credit for it." At that point in the conversation, his eyes got misty. Joey had never been around soldiers in his life, but if there was one common trait that he had heard about them, it was that they never shed tears publicly; they never allowed their emotions to get the best of them. The immigrant patted the brave military man on his back and said, "Thank you for sharing your inspiring story with me. Your grandfather and your uncle must be proud of you in heaven. Everything will be alright."

In his sixty-something years, Major Brown had endured a whole lot due to the systemic racism in the United States and telling his story to Joey was like reliving every scene all over again, and it would be hard for even the devil to remain dry-faced through all of that.

After a moment, he pulled himself together and said, "Look here young man, now that you will be driving around on your own and you just got to this country, I feel like I would be failing you if, as your occasional driving instructor, I didn't give you the full picture about driving in America as a Black male. You've to be extra careful on these roads. You're going to be pulled over by the police and the highway patrol more often than White people, and most of the time it will be for nothing; you will just be guilty of driving while Black, which happens to be a very serious offense for some White cops in this country. What you do whenever you get stopped by one of these devils in uniform will determine whether you head to your home or to the funeral home."

Those blunt words shook Joey to his core. He was terrified. "You mean the police could kill me just for being a Black man behind a steering wheel?"

"Yes, exactly! And that has happened tens of thousands of times, more than 300 times this year already."

"Oh, my God! That's scary!"

"When you get stopped, and that day will come very soon, just make sure to keep your hands on the wheel and within view of the officer or officers the entire time and do exactly as told. No sudden movements or else you're dead. When they ask for your license and registration, ask them if you could reach for your wallet or the glove compartment for these documents, and then, do so slowly, while telling and reminding them what you're doing. When you find what they asked for, hand it to them, again slowly, respectfully, and politely, even when they are rude, aggressive, insulting, and violent. You must remain calm, compliant, and obedient to preserve your life. It's absolutely important to leave the scene alive in order to fight your case in court some other day, although the courts almost always side with the police officers, even when they brutally murder an innocent, defenseless Black driver. Never try to resist, fight back, question, or reason with them as it will only anger them and increase the likelihood of you being shot. It's true that on thousands of occasions, Black people, mostly males, have acted obediently and respectfully when they have been pulled over by White cops, but they have still wound up getting killed, however, your chances of being shot increase exponentially if you don't do what they tell you to do. So, do anything you can to keep the temperature down so that you can survive the police stop."

Joey was petrified. He wondered if he should just take the

car back to the dealership, because it looked like driving was an exceptionally dangerous activity for Black people in America. But the thought of giving up his earned freedom out of fear of some degenerate cops was enough for him to conclude that he would take his chances with the police officers, with heightened precautions though.

"One last thing, if you ever get pulled over at night, you want to make sure that you keep driving until you get to a well-lit place. It would reduce the chances of the cops doing something nefarious to you," Major Brown added.

"Thank you so much for having this talk with me. I really appreciate it, even though I have never heard anything scarier than what you have told me today. I hope the anxiety and fear of cops that I am feeling right now doesn't handicap the quality of my driving on these streets and interstates."

"I hope that doesn't happen either. You don't want to give them the slightest reason to come for you. Always remember, Joey, that unlike the Black Americans born in this country who are just hated because of the color of their skin, you have two strikes against you, or what some would call double jeopardy: not only are you a Black male, but you are also an immigrant. Therefore, they will hate you both for being Black and for not being from here. You will be a victim of both racism and xenophobia. So, you've to be extra careful on these roads and everywhere you go. You're an impressively smart Black immigrant male with tremendous potential to go very far in life in America, and that makes you uniquely exposed and vulnerable. That's why it's important for you to be aware of these things and to intentionally take appropriate steps to protect yourself. I wouldn't want anything bad to happen to you, son."

By the time they separated, Joey was so mortified that he was not exactly sure if driving himself around was still an option he wanted to pursue. Maybe he should just keep depending on his friends for rides to places, at least until he could get over the fright that the talk with Major Brown had instilled in him.

"No, the only way to overcome the fear would be to confront it head on!" he chided himself.

CHAPTER FIVE

UNDETERRED

The rest of that school year was great, for the most part. Joey progressively acquired firm control of his classes, thus significantly improving teaching and learning. During his planning period as well as on his spare time at home, he would read voraciously about innovative instructional strategies and best practices in the teaching of both English and foreign languages in high schools. That was how he learned about Fisher and Frey's Gradual Release of Responsibility model of teaching and Webb's Depth of Knowledge concepts. He combined these theories to enhance the rigor, engagement, and critical thinking of his lessons on the one hand, and to boost collaborative and independent learning on the other hand.

His students initially resisted the increased struggle that the enhanced rigor and higher order thinking brought to his classes, but he soon got them and their parents to buy in to the concept of productive struggle in effective learning. By the end of the school year, the kids' respective reading levels had improved by at least two points on average. Additionally, the clarity and fluency of their speaking and writing saw significant improvements.

His personal life too was blossoming. He went on multiple dates with Emily and hung out with some of her friends, most of whom were members of Teach for America like her. They were in cities all over the Mississippi Delta.

One Saturday in early May, she asked him if he didn't mind

going with her to a birthday party that one of her friends was throwing at her place in Greenville.

"I'll go with you. I don't have anything planned for this weekend, and besides, I could use some party entertainment," he responded.

They arrived at the venue of the celebration at 7:30 pm. It was a huge white and yellow house on the left side of the street as soon as they turned on Washington Avenue from Highway 82. There were at least 6 bedrooms in the old mansion, an imposing and majestic edifice that was probably constructed in the early days of the 20th century.

Emily's friend, Anne, the birthday girl, lived in the house with 7 other teachers, all White and in their early to mid-twenties. Standing about 5'6" and weighing about 240 lbs., she had short blonde hair, green eyes, and a particularly long nose.

Emily introduced her man to her friend.

"Nice to finally meet you, Joey! I've heard a lot about you," Anne said

"It's a pleasure meeting you," Joey responded.

"I hear you're from Africa. How long have you been in our country?" she asked.

The conspicuous possessive pronoun in the question and the speaker's intention to otherize him did not escape Joey. He played along.

"Yes, I'm from Africa, precisely from Cameroon, and I've been in YOUR country since January this year." He made sure to put the emphasis on the possessive pronoun in his response.

"That's awesome! And how long are you going to be here?"

Joey did not like where the conversation was going, but he had no problem facing what looked like a disgusting, racist xenophobe.

"Well, my visa will expire at the end of this month, and I'll have to return home a few days before that happens or risk being deported," he lied.

He had an H1B Visa that was good for three years, and it was renewable, with the possibility of eventually making him eligible for permanent residency, a status that also opened the way to US citizenship down the road.

"I see! But if you get married to an American citizen, you will not have to leave. That's why you're with my friend, isn't it? You're a very smart guy!" she exclaimed excitedly, with such confidence and smile like those of someone who had just singlehandedly figured out the answer to a puzzling problem that everyone had been attempting to solve for a long time. She was conspicuously amused by what she was doing. Emily was livid, and she was about to pounce to her man's rescue when he responded, as clearly and sternly as he could, given the circumstances, "Let me tell you something, ma'am, I don't understand what your problem is, but you're not going to make inferences and draw conclusions about me when you don't even know me. I find that exceptionally disrespectful, and you're not going to disrespect me, not here in your home, not anywhere!"

Unfortunately for Anne, Joey's voice only got louder as he continued speaking, and more and more people were starting to get interested in finding out what was going on right at the main entrance to the residence.

The fuming exchange teacher continued, "Just so you know, I can stay in the United States for as long as I want to, if I want to. I don't need to get married to an American citizen or get anyone's help to do that. I'm an exchange teacher, and the visa that I have is renewable every three years, with the possibility of getting a green card and becoming a US citizen several years after that. It's disgusting that you harbor such sick, racist, and xenophobic ideas about someone you've never met. You're crazy to think that I'm using your friend as my ticket to stay in YOUR COUNTRY."

With that, he turned to his girlfriend and asked if she was ready to leave. He did not need to ask as she had lost the desire to be at the event the very moment that her friend mentioned "...OUR COUNTRY." Before they exited, Emily made sure she emphasized one last point clearly enough, "Listen, Anne, it's my damn choice to be with whomever I want: White, Black, Asian, Hispanic, or whatever. You need to stay out of my fucking business and start minding yours!"

They headed to a bar, Garfield's, in the Greenville shopping mall. On the way there, Emily apologized for taking Joey to the toxic birthday party.

"I'm sorry JJ! I didn't know that Anne was prejudiced and xenophobic like that. I just can't believe that she said all those things to you! I was going to give her a piece of my mind because I was extremely offended by everything she said, but you didn't let me."

"That's okay, babe. I wanted to stand up for myself. I've taken those hateful remarks and comments from people in this country quietly for too long."

They had a few drinks at the bar that Saturday night until 12:00 am, then they went home, more in love and tighter than ever.

Joey was very happy when school finally dismissed for the summer on May 25th as he would have all the time he needed to carefully find his own place to stay. The first property for rent that he found was a single-family house on Chapman Street, in a particularly clean and quiet neighborhood in Indianola. It had three bedrooms, two full baths, a two-car garage, and a good size kitchen. Additionally, the hardwood floors were gleaming and flowed from the vaulted entrance all through the house. Also, there were new appliances in the kitchen and in the laundry room, while the living room and the bedrooms were all fully furnished. The red brick exterior walls were very clean for an older house. They must have been pressure-washed recently. Similarly, the cream interior walls still spread fresh paint smell that hit Joey as soon as he got to the driveway.

If he got the house, the only thing that he would need to purchase would be kitchen utensils, plates, and silverware. The very affordable lease was $675.00 a month. He would not need to find roommates to split the rent with.

He dialed the number that was on the yard sign, and a female answered.

"Hello!"

"Yes, hello! My name is Joey, and I'm calling about the house for rent on Chapman. Is it still available?"

"Oh yes! Yes, it's available. This is Sara Jefferson and me and my husband, Rudy, own the property, by the way. When are you available to take a look?"

"I can be there in 30 minutes, if that's fine with you," Joey suggested.

"Let's meet in an hour. I'm in Greenwood, and I need to wrap up what I'm doing before I can get on the road. Does that work for you?"

"Yes, ma'am! I'll see you in one hour."

"What do you do for a living, if you don't mind me asking?"

"I'm a high school teacher. I teach French and English at Gentry High."

"Okay, that's nice, that's nice!"

He could not wait to get over to the house for the appointment. He was already dreaming up a thousand things that he was going to do in the house after moving in. For instance, he was thinking about the types of decoration for each room, how to rearrange the furniture that came with the rental property, where he would place his TV and stereo sets, etc. His friends would be welcome to spend the night whenever they wanted. He could even throw a few parties in the huge, beautiful backyard in the spring and in the summer if he wanted to. So many ideas were racing through his mind as he was driving, excitedly and with great anticipation, to meet the landlady.

He made it to the place on time. There was a white Mercury Grand Marquis in the wide, concrete driveway with two people in it. He parked right behind them and alighted.

An elderly White man came out of the front passenger side of the Grand Marquis, followed by the driver, a White lady in her eighties. She was shorter than him. Her white linen, short sleeve top and Capri pants of similar color and fabric matched her almost snow-white short hair. Dark spots of various sizes could be seen on the exposed parts of her skin. The couple stood in front of their car as Joey approached.

"Good afternoon, Mrs. Jefferson. I'm Joey, we spoke on the phone about an hour ago," he said as he warmly extended his hand for a handshake. The lady did not reciprocate. Instead, she turned to her husband, a very frail looking fellow who was dressed in an oversized flowery Hawaiian shirt and khaki pants that clearly were made to fit someone two sizes bigger. His Jesus sandals revealed his pale skin and green crisscrossing veins, just like on his wrinkled face. The hair on his head was patchy and several abrasions could be seen in the bald areas.

An uncomfortably palpable silence ensued for what seemed like ten minutes, then, leaning heavily on his cane, Mr. Jefferson said in a shaky, raspy voice, "This house is not for rent anymore." Joey was shocked. That was not possible. The lady had just told him less than 70 minutes earlier that the house was available, and she had invited him to tour the premises. It was hard to believe that the couple would have driven all the way from Greenwood to get to Indianola at the time of the appointment if they were not coming to meet a potential tenant.

"Something else must be going on," Joey thought, and he was determined to get to the bottom of it.

"I don't understand, sir! I just spoke to your wife about an hour ago, and she assured me that this house was available for rent, and she set up this appointment. She even told me to bring my checkbook to pay the deposit and first month's rent, if I liked the place."

As Joey was speaking, confused, he was trying to make eye contact with Mrs. Jefferson, but she kept looking away the whole time, and she even attempted at one point to walk away.

"Well, hmm, hmm, hmm," the old man could not find his words. He cleared his throat at least thrice, still trying to find the words to verbalize how he felt, a feeling that seemed to get caught in his throat each time it tried to make it to his lips.

He gave it one more forceful attempt, and finally, some of the most racist and most hateful words Joey had ever heard since arriving in the United States came out of Mr. Jefferson's mouth. "Well, the thing is, I don't know how to put this, because I don't mean no offense and no harm, but we don't rent to your kind. Don't get me wrong now, we're not racist. We love Black people. Many of our friends over the years have been Black. Our children have Black friends too that they went to school and worked with. There are Black people in our church, and we're happy to worship with them every Sunday."

Joey was astounded and speechless, not because of what was happening before his eyes. He had already witnessed racism on many occasions. So, an old racist White man in the Mississippi Delta expressing his disdain for Black people was not particularly surprising to him, given the dark history of the region. What was appalling to him was the fact that the couple hated people like him so passionately that they were willing to turn down a decent and reliable tenant with money and keep their rental property vacant until a White tenant came along. Until that moment in the driveway, he always thought that when it came to doing things that were financially beneficial to them, racist people would be willing to deal with individuals outside their race.

"Okay, thank you sir! I'm sorry I made you drive all the way over here for nothing. I hope you find the type of tenant you prefer for your property very soon," Joey said, as devoid of sarcasm as he could before he drove away.

He immediately called Emily to tell her what had just transpired, and she suggested reporting the couple to the Indianola Chamber of Commerce and to the mayor's office. The couple needed to be called out, she said. When he made it home, both of them called Major Brown for guidance on the matter. He told them that, while he agreed with them that what the Jeffersons did was incredibly deplorable and reprehensible, he would not advise them to waste their time reporting them because White landlords had been discriminating against minorities locally and nationally for centuries with absolute impunity. He added that the couple could also deny saying that they did not rent their house to Blacks, and no one could prove otherwise; it would just be their word against Joey's.

"Just don't waste your time fighting these White people. They control everything over here: the good properties, the money, the law, the businesses, the law makers, the government, and so on. Keep looking around, and you will find you a good place to stay very soon," he added.

Two days later, he was jogging down Catchings Avenue, heading to the park behind the hospital, when he saw a "For Rent" sign in the window of a house on the right side of the road. It was a cabin-style construction, clean and pretty on the exterior, with a chain-link fence on the right side of the property, separating it from another residence of similar architecture. It did not have a garage, but the long driveway was great for parking several vehicles. A red brick walkway went from the right edge of the driveway to the three steps that led to a veranda and to the front door. The front and the backyard were same size and similarly sodded. Both were adorned with roses, daisies, lilies, and other flowers growing in beds located in the center of the lawn. 211 Catchings was not perfectly located like the house he wanted on Chapman, but he liked it. Emily and his friends would be down the street from him, and his commute time to work would not change. He would be able to continue his daily workout routine at the park as well.

He called the number on the sign, and the caretaker, Mr. Jackson, asked him if he wanted a tour right away as he happened to be doing some renovation work in the house. Just like the other house, the rental property he was invited to see had three bedrooms and two bathrooms, but there were a few significant differences: there was tan carpet everywhere, except in the kitchen and the bathrooms where the floors were vinyl. Additionally, the interior walls were made with brown wood paneling. He would also need to buy furniture for the bedrooms, living room, and kitchen as the landlord was not providing anything beyond the standard stove and refrigerator. If he wanted to do laundry at home, he would need to buy a washer and a dryer too. However, 211 Catchings was much cheaper, just $375.00 monthly, and with the savings from the rent, he could progressively purchase the things that he needed for his place.

Mr. Jackson, a 6'5", 215 lbs., broad-chested, and muscular Black guy with long, thick fingers did not have any hair on his head. It was skin-bald and reminded Joey of the fellow in the Mr. Clean commercial on TV. He was waiting for Joey on the veranda.

The landlord, a very rich White businessman, lived in Jackson, MS, but Mr. Jackson had permission to handle the paperwork for the 27 rental properties that he owned in the Delta. According to Mr. Jackson, the landlord owned houses and apartments for rent in every county in the state of Mississippi and more in other major cities around the United States.

The renovations were completed within 48 hours and Joey was able for sign his lease agreement and gain possession of the keys to his new dwelling. With his own place thus secured, he shopped around for a few necessary pieces of furniture to get started. At a furniture store on Highway 82, he was turned down for financing because he "... did not have sufficient credit." However, the owner of the store told him that he would let him have the furniture he needed through a special financing program that they had for people like him, but the interest rate was 29.99%. To lessen the impact of the excruciating loan terms, Joey paid a significant amount upfront and committed to doubling or even tripling the monthly note until the furniture was paid off. He would have had enough money to buy what he needed if he had not sent money back home the day before to assist his father with a medical emergency. Thus, he purchased the basics, including furniture for his bedroom, a couch and a TV for the living room and a breakfast table with four chairs for the kitchen.

His former roommates, Andy, Emily, and Josh helped him move into his house and even threw a small house-warming celebration for him. Other close friends and colleagues brought gifts that comprised of kitchen and bathroom utensils.

Joey was incredibly thankful for everything that his former roommates had done for him since his arrival in Indianola. Friends like them were extremely rare, especially in a city with a worldwide reputation of overt racism. They had opened their doors to a Black stranger that they knew nothing about and had let him stay with them four months longer than they had initially agreed, all out of the kindness of their hearts. In April, they had told him that he was welcome to stay with them the next school year and even beyond that if he wanted, but he believed that their friendship would be even stronger with a certain distance between them, because he had learned from past experiences and from his readings that too much familiarity often ruined great friendships. In fact, growing up in Cameroon, there was a common saying that good neighbors mend tall fences in order not to get too familiar with and lose respect for each other in the process.

With his own place to stay and a car to go wherever he needed to, Joey was thus totally independent. He was ecstatic about his accomplishments, even though they came at a significant price, literally. In less than six months in America, he had accomplished what would not have been possible for decades in Cameroon, and that made him proud and hopeful. Despite the challenges he had encountered and the ones he knew the road ahead was littered with, he looked forward to the journey with tremendous optimism and great anticipation.

The day after Joey moved out of the house that they had been sharing with him since his arrival in January that year, his roommates took off for their respective home-towns to spend the summer. Because they did not want their daughter to travel alone, and due to the fact that they had never seen where she had been teaching for a couple of years, Emily's parents took a road trip to Indianola to pick her up.

At 1:00 pm on that day, Joey got call from Emily asking if he would like to join her and her parents for lunch at Lost Dog, the new restaurant across from Walmart on Highway 82. She had told him countless stories about her parents and her life growing up with them when they had started dating, and she had promised to introduce him to them whenever the first opportunity presented itself. There it was, and he could not hesitate to meet them. He often heard her talk about him to them whenever they would call, but they never asked to speak to him, and she never brought it up either. However, everything indicated that they were very nice people. "Only impressive parents could raise a remarkably caring and kind daughter like Emily, and it would be an immense honor to meet them," he said to himself as he looked for an empty parking spot between the restaurant and another business.

He arrived at Lost Dog just as the waiter was seating Emily and her parents. She waved to get his attention, and he excitedly hurried to the table. Sitting directly opposite from her mother on one end of the four-seat table was her father, a very handsome sharply dressed gentleman. On top of his white, modern fit, button-down shirt was a Ralph Lauren, gold and blue plaid sportscoat that fit him perfectly and highlighted his mannequinlike features. The coat went well with his navy-blue pants and brown Salvatore Ferragamo loafers. On his left wrist was an impressive gold Rolex with a blue dial that matched his pants, while on his right wrist was a brown, braided leather bracelet, the exact same color as his shoes. The two top buttons of his shirt were unbuttoned, thus revealing a gorgeous necklace with a crafted compass pendant. It was obvious that the man cared about his looks and took time to ensure that everything he wore was carefully coordinated.

His equally fit and attractive wife matched his taste for fine fashion. Her sleeveless blue lace skater dress had a v-neckline that highlighted her collarbone and gave her a distinctive appearance. Her beautiful diamond necklace with a gold and diamond pendant matched the mixture of gold and diamond bracelets that she wore on her right hand as well as the diamond Gucci watch that was on her left wrist. On her feet was a pair of navy micro block-heel platform sandals with adjustable ankle straps.

Emily's parents made a fabulous couple, and they looked like money. Joey did not think that they were even close to the 55 years that she said both were. To say that he was blown away by their appearance would be an understatement. Luckily enough for him, he was not underdressed for the occasion. He wore a Joseph Abboud navy blue sportscoat on top of a white Charles Tyrwhitt button down shirt that went well with his tan, modern fit Tommy Hilfiger pants and brown Magnanni Chaplin leather bit loafers. He was not at the Rolex level, but his $250 Michael Kors watch with brown leather straps complemented his outfit just fine.

By the time that Joey got to the table, the waiter who had sat the family had retreated, and, believing that the male approaching them was a member of the waiting staff, Emily's mother yelled to him, "We're not ready to order yet. We're still expecting one more person to join us. As soon as he makes it, we'll be ready. Emily, could you describe Joey to this fine gentleman so that he would be brought to our table as soon as he arrives?"

Joey was amused. He felt the high regard that he had developed for his girlfriend's parent take a precipitous decline.

"Why would she mistake me for a waiter? Do I look like one, or is it because I'm Black?" he wondered. "She can't be a racist, no way! She's Emily's mother, and she doesn't have a single racist bone in her body!" he continued, but what happened next just completely knocked him befuddled.

"Mom, this is Joey," yelled Emily. She sounded like someone who was embarrassed by what had just happened.

"What! You did not tell us that he is Black!" her mother responded, loudly enough that patrons sitting 10 feet away heard her. Both parents had a stunned and disappointed look on their face, like they had just found out something disgusting and abhorrent about their precious daughter.

Emily gasped and almost collapsed. In just a few weeks, she had witnessed several racist and xenophobic individuals say the most hurtful and hateful things to her boyfriend, and on each occasion, she had stood up to defend him, but the fact that her own mother was the one saying something so racist about her lover was exceptionally humiliating and debilitating.

There was an uneasy silence at the table for what seemed like hours, with Joey still standing. He had not even had a chance to utter a word of greeting when things took a totally unexpected turn.

His lady stood up, right next to him, her palm tightly covering her mouth, tears streaming down her cheeks. Her right hand reached for his left hand and his five fingers locked into hers tightly. He could feel her trembling feverishly. He was trying to find the right words to say. He knew her so well, and he understood that she was deeply ashamed and embarrassed. For the second time in their short relationship, she had exposed her sweetheart to racism, and the sting of that was immensely painful to her.

"It's okay, honey," he whispered in her ear. "It's okay!"

"No, it's not okay!" she responded angrily, and added emphatically, still shaking, "Mom, Dad, Joey is the love of my life. We've been dating for more than four months. He treats me far better than anyone has ever treated me. If you have a problem with the fact that he's Black, then you've a problem with me! Joey and I are deeply in love, and we're not going to break up because you don't like me dating a Black man." The pitch of her voice inclined with each word that came out of her mouth.

"JJ, I apologize for my parents, and I know that it'll be hard for you to sit and eat with them after such an embarrassing treatment. If you want to leave, I would truly understand, and I would leave with you," she said firmly.

"No, we're not leaving. Everything'll be alright. I believe that your parents will appreciate and respect me when they get to know the content of my character," he replied, strategically extending his hand toward her father for a handshake. Because he hadn't said a word since the drama started, Joey suspected that he might be the good cop in the couple, and he could be instrumental in defusing the situation.

"It's a pleasure meeting you, Mr. Goldman. Emily has told me so many amazing things about you. I can't count the number of times she has told me stories about fishing trips with you on your boat and memories of you teaching her how to save money and track her daily expenditure on a spreadsheet since she was five years old. Sometimes she forgets that she has told me the same stories time and time again, but I just pretend that I'm hearing them for the first time, you know. To her, you're the greatest man on the face of this planet."

Joey had guessed right. His words were tugging at Emily's father's heart strings. He pulled a handkerchief from his pocket and wiped the tears that suddenly welled in his eyes as he heard the level of regard that his daughter had for him.

"She's our sweet little girl, our only child, the greatest joy of our life, and we dream of only the best for her," he responded after shaking Joey's hand warmly and gesturing for him to take the empty seat at the table.

Before sitting, Joey reached for a handshake with Mrs. Goldman and said, "It's an immense honor to finally meet you, ma'am," as honestly as he could, even though he did not really mean a word of what he said. Emily moved her chair to the same side of the table as her sweetheart and placed it so close to his that the two seats made them look like they were joined at the hip.

The mood at the table eased progressively during lunch, aided tremendously by the alcohol that everyone, especially the parents, was drinking.

Mr. Goldman inquired about Cameroon, Joey's family, his educational trajectory, and what brought him to the United States, pretty much the same questions that Joey had been asked a million times daily by different people everywhere he went. He was pleasantly surprised that Mr. Goldman did know a lot about the dictatorship and the systemic corruption in Cameroon as well as the economic crisis and the AIDS pandemic in Africa at large. At the mention of the latter, Mrs. Goldman asked if Africans are systematically screened for HIV before they are allowed into the United States.

"Not all the time, but if you're wondering if I've been tested, then, yes, I've tested negative twice in the past 11 months," Joey hammered.

The malice and disdain in her question was not unperceived by him, but he chose to ignore it, preferring to focus on the positive. Emily was happy he did. Her mother would come around. Consistent positive vibes would eventually suffocate the negativity in her, he thought.

Lunch ended peacefully, and Mr. Goldman even invited his daughter's boyfriend to Bear, Delaware for his annual 4th of July party.

They returned to Emily's place one last time and Joey loaded her luggage and her parents' belongings into her car. Then, they hugged and kissed, hugged, and kissed again and again, like they were not going to see each other for a very long time.

"That's enough! You both will see each other again in a few weeks. Save some for later," her father yelled from behind the steering wheel.

"I love you, pretty. I'll see you on July 4th," he said and kissed her one more time. He opened the door and let her into the back seat of the car, kissed her again and slowly closed it.

As the car drove off, she lowered the window and yelled, "I'll call you every hour until we make it to Delaware," then she blew him kisses multiple times, and he reciprocated.

Back home, alone and with nothing to do, he started reflecting on the unexpectedly shocking encounter with his girlfriend's parents. If there were any White people who he could have predicted would be pro-racial diversity and interracial dating, it would have been Emily's parents, because of what he knew about her. He had wrongly assumed that, if Emily could be so kindhearted toward everyone, regardless of their gender, race, sexual orientation, religion, etc., then she could only have been taught that by parents who were diversity friendly and heterogeneity-conscious themselves. That assumption was partly informed by the common saying he had heard all his life that, "The apple doesn't fall far from the tree" and "Like mother, like daughter," but sadly, in his lady's case, he discovered that the apple fell thousands of miles from the producing tree. In fact, the fruit did not seem to have anything in common with its progenitor. Emily was nothing like her racist, xenophobic, hateful, and ignorant mother.

Joey concluded that, from that day onward, he would not assume anything about anyone; he would simply approach everyone with extreme caution until they proved to be worthy of his time, friendship, trust, and interaction.

The heated meeting with the Goldmans also cemented his love and admiration for Emily. If she was willing to abandon her parents in a restaurant in a city they did not know because they had disrespected her man, then he would never leave her, at least not without a very solidly grounded reason. His enhanced attachment to her gave him another valid reason to stay in the United States. He had no doubt that she would move to Cameroon or anywhere else with him without hesitating if it were necessary, but circumstances in his home country warranted making his life in the United States regardless of the certain, predictable challenges ahead.

With the decision to stay in America came thoughts of how to enhance his career and life. He concluded that he would need to further his education to increase his chances of advancing professionally. An American advanced degree would also boost his income, and he would be better placed to one day provide for his wife and kids and for his family back home in Cameroon.

Since he had obtained a master's degree in education in Cameroon, he enrolled in a doctoral program in educational leadership at Delta State University in Cleveland, MS, the week after Emily left. If everything went as he carefully thought, he would become a school administrator and teach at a university as an adjunct after graduating in three to four years.

While he was at Delta State for enrollment, the doctoral program coordinator told him about some Cameroonians that she knew in Memphis, TN, less than three hours away. She even gave him the phone number of one of them, a pilot with FedEx, and one Saturday in June Joey called the number, and the guy, Sam Fominyam, answered.

Joey was talking to someone from his home country, and for anyone who has ever travelled to a foreign land, speaking to a fellow countryman for the first time provokes a special feeling that words cannot describe. It's almost like speaking to a lost family member after a very long time. Coincidentally, Sam was also from Mbengwi where Joey was born and bred. He told him that there was a huge Cameroonian community in Memphis and that their monthly gathering was occurring that same Saturday at 5:00 pm at the home of one of their members. He asked if Joey would like to be a guest at the meeting.

"Absolutely. I'd be delighted to come."

"You could spend the night at my place after the meeting, if it's too late for you to drive back to, where did you say you live again?"

"Indianola, Mississippi."

"Yes, if it's too late for you to return to Indianola, you could spend the night at my house and just leave on Sunday morning. I'll tell my wife so she can prepare the guest room for you."

"That's so kind of you. Thank you very much! Let me get ready so I can be there on time. Please don't forget to text me your address."

He was extremely excited when he got off the phone with Sam, and he was particularly eager to meet his fellow countrymen and women in a few hours. He could not wait to find out about their individual and collective experiences in Uncle Sam's country.

CHAPTER SIX

NOT ALONE

To get to Memphis from Indianola, Joey took the 448 to Cleveland before getting on Highway 61 which offered a straight route to the Bluff City. Because his foot was not light on the gas pedal, he made it to Sam's residence on Quince in 2.5 hours. His host, who was standing in his yard, pointed to a spot for Joey to park his Nissan Maxima.

Sam, a tall, slim, and very dark-skinned 45-year-old Cameroonian with a neat bald fade haircut and a perfectly trimmed moustache and goatee, lived in an immense piece of modern architecture with his wife and two children. The five-bedroom and four-bathroom house also featured a three-car garage, a beautiful sunroom in the back, an outdoor entertainment area with a built-in grill, a bar, and a spacious sitting area across from a swimming pool.

After giving Joey a tour of the premises and showing him the guestroom to place his overnight luggage, Sam's wife, Lilian, also from Mbengwi, asked if he wanted something to drink before they left for Olive Branch, MS to attend the meeting. She was not slim-built and athletic like her husband, but Lilian looked like she cared a great deal about her appearance. She seemed a little younger than Sam, probably in her mid-thirties. She fixed an excellent old fashioned for Joey and told him that was her husband's favorite as well.

Thirty minutes later, Sam was driving Joey in his Mercedes S Class to Olive Branch, a suburb on the border of Tennessee and Mississippi. During the 20-minute ride, they chatted about Mbengwi, their families, life in America and much more. They found out that they had both attended the same primary and secondary schools more than 10 years apart, Government Bilingual School and Government High School Mbengwi respectively. There were still dozens of people in the town that they both knew, and talking about them caused very strong feelings of nostalgia, especially for Sam who had not been home in six years due to his hectic work schedule.

"So, how long have you lived in the United States, Sam?"

"25 years. I came here to go to college, and after that, I joined the Air Force, became a pilot while in service for 10 years. At the time, I lived in Maryland."

"That's quite impressive. So how did you end up in Memphis?"

"Well, while I was an Air Force pilot, I met a guy who was one of the directors at FedEx during a mission to Okinawa, Japan, and he told me about all the amazing benefits that their pilots were afforded. He told me to give him a call if I left the military and was interested in flying cargo planes. One year later, at the end of my 10th year of service, I decided to get out. My career was not progressing as I deserved, and I was tired of seeing airmen with less credentials and experience than me being promoted every year, while I was overlooked because of my race and because I was an immigrant. So, I checked out FedEx and saw that they were hiring experienced pilots. I applied, completed the required training process and the rest is history."

"That's an incredible story. It's surprising to me that there would be racial discrimination in the most powerful military in the world, given how counterproductive and demoralizing that could be for the affected soldiers in times of conflict."

Sam burst out laughing, profusely.

"Racism has existed in the United States military ever since Blacks were first allowed to serve, more than a century ago. At the time, racial discrimination was overtly systemic, but these days, it's very subtle, because, in theory, there are laws prohibiting discrimination of any kind in the military."

"It must have been very devastating to be discriminated against because of the color of your skin and because you're not from here."

"It was debilitating, I tell you, my brother! The worst part was that people, often my supervisors, would tell me to go back to Africa if I didn't like what was happening to me. Some said that I should be happy to have made it as far as I had in the Air Force. But enough about me. I'm sure you've seen all forms of racism and xenophobia in Mississippi, the place that's known worldwide for the lynching of people for the color of their skin."

"Absolutely. I've only been there for six months, but what I've experienced is incredibly disgusting. I don't even know where to start. For instance, my very first week teaching at my school, I went to the main office to complete some paperwork and the secretary, a Black lady for that matter, was pissed that the school district had hired an African. She did not like the fact that Africans come over here to take their jobs."

"I've been told that by both Whites and Blacks, at least once every week for 25 years now, even here in Memphis, so get used to it, bro!"

"Oh yes! That wasn't the only time though. The following week, a PE teacher, a Black guy who I found out later was banging the secretary, told me that Africans like me were the reason why there were so many Americans without jobs. He insisted that I go back to my country. You know, the first two times that happened, I didn't respond; I calmly completed what I had to do and walked away, but after some time, I decided the next time someone said something that stupid to me, I would give them a piece of my African mind. Black immigrants in this county endure a lot at the hands of some ignorant and evil Whites and from some insane and hypocritical so-called Black brothers and sisters. We suffer racism and xenophobia from Whites, and, the people that we would assume would be understanding toward us because of our common ancestry, don't treat us any better. Ironically, when February comes around annually, and they're having Black History programs in the schools, churches, and organizations left and right, they suddenly start seeking Africans, like bees craving nectar, to speak at their events or to obtain authentic traditional regalia and other African artifacts to showcase at the events, like they're very proud of their African heritage. How pathetic is that? Last February 18th, the secretary at my school had the audacity to tell my former roommate to ask me if I could be the keynote speaker at a Black history program at her church. I naively accepted, hoping that it would endear me in her eyes. She was nice to me for a week after the event, then less than a score days later she turned frosty toward me."

"That's some crazy shit, but it doesn't surprise me. I'll introduce you to other Cameroonians at the gathering, and when you hear their stories, you'd understand that you have huge company in your misery. Sometimes we've Nigerians, Ivorians, Congolese, Tanzanians, and immigrants from many other African countries at these meetings. Their experiences all seem to be pages pulled from the same book."

The venue of the meeting was the home of another Cameroonian, Jonas Werenge, a physician with the Methodist hospital in Memphis.

To bring together Cameroonians in the Midsouth, including Arkansas, Mississippi, and Tennessee, a handful of pioneers created the organization called CAMSUS, short for Cameroonians of the Midsouth, a decade earlier. By 2009, it had grown to more than a hundred active members who came together monthly, in a rotary manner, at the home of a different countryman or woman on the first Saturday of the month. The meetings were thus spaced to give the host ample time to find and prepare Cameroonian delicacies like achu, eru, ndole, kondre, kahti-kahti, koki, etc. Early on the day of the meeting, some ladies in the group would converge at the home of the host to assist with the cooking and setting up of the décor. Additional food and drinks would be brought by the rest of the ladies and gentlemen respectively later when the meeting started. The drinks, mostly alcohol of all shades, colors, and brands, even some from Cameroon, combined with the traditional cuisine, would spark nostalgic feelings and conversations among the attendees.

The first part of the meeting, typically presided over by the elected president, consisted of a reading of the minutes from the previous session by the secretary, updates on outstanding matters such as community projects, scholarships, healthcare assistance, and other humanitarian initiatives that the group was involved in locally in the United States and in Cameroon. Following that would be the announcement of the host of the next get-together. The person was usually picked from a list of volunteers and collected funds for food and drinks would be handed to him or her. With all the key matters closed, a volunteer would be called up to bless the food and drinks thus opening item 11. Everyone would then eat and drink as much as they wanted. There would be so much left over, even after people would have gone for seconds and thirds and packed some to-go.

Later in the night, when everyone would have eaten to their fill, the floor would open for dancing, mostly to Cameroonian music, to dance-off all the calories consumed. Attendees would dance and eat and drink some more all night until Sunday morning. Newcomers would often use that time to meet and interact with other attendees.

Joey's first experience at a CAMSUS meeting did not disappoint. The spread of the different types of Cameroonian dishes was overwhelming to him. He had never seen that much food, that many varieties, and that amount of alcohol in one place his whole life. Additionally, he had not eaten or drunk anything Cameroonian since he left home six months earlier. Thus, he tried a little bit of everything and, when the time came to dance, his legs just could not handle the weight of his stomach. The six shots of Remy Martin that he had drunk since arriving at the event had complicated things further, thus robbing him of his balance. He excused himself to his dance partner, an extremely beautiful and seductively dressed lady who had asked him to join her on the dance floor when the loudspeakers started blasting "Battoh" by Cameroonian superstar, Petit Pays. She was not disappointed; in fact, she helped him to his seat and fetched a bottle for water for him.

"Drink this, it'll help you," the attractive lady with a voluptuous bosom and a curvy posterior said.

"Thank you so much! My name is Joey by the way."

"Nice to meet you, Joey. I'm Solange. Is it your first time at a CAMSUS meeting? I don't think I've ever seen you at any of the past ones."

He did not know if it was the effect of the alcohol or not, but it looked like her breasts were about to pop out of the black, body-hugging dress that she had on. They seemed to bounce at each word that came out of her mouth. She sure was the type of female that any man would look at more than twice.

"Yes," he responded.

"That means you don't live in Memphis, because all Cameroonians in the Bluff City are either members or visit from time to time. So, where're you based?"

"You're right. I live in Indianola, MS."

"Oh wow! I know where that is; it's in the Delta, isn't it? One of the most rural places in the United States. What made you move out there?"

"I didn't have a choice; my exchange teacher program sent me to Indianola."

"That's interesting! What do you think about the place?"

"For the most part, it's been okay. Most of the people there are incredibly hospitable and nice. I love the soul food restaurants around the Delta as they remind me of Cameroonian cuisine. Also, life is very inexpensive there, although the pay is kind of proportionate. Additionally, because the place is so small, everything is within walking distance, thus making for fast errands, even when one doesn't want to drive. However, the flipside of the size of my city, Indianola, is that one must be creative to have a private life. I run into my colleagues, students, and their parents everywhere I go. And you, what do you do for a living?"

"I'm an ER physician at a hospital here in Memphis. I've been to the Delta a couple of times to see a Cameroonian brother who used to be a doctor at King's Daughters Hospital in Greenville. He was attracted there by the cost of living and, mostly, by the critical shortage of physicians in the area. That appealed to his immense desire to help communities in dire need of highly qualified healthcare providers. Unfortunately, he left after just two years of service because of the glaring cases of racism that he either witnessed or was a victim of on a frequent basis. Have you experienced any of that where you live?"

"Of course, it would be hard to find a Black person in Mississippi who hasn't experienced racism firsthand. The chances of that happening to you increase exponentially if you are both Black and immigrant. From common occurrences like being told frequently to 'go back to your shithole country in Africa,' to people standing up and moving to other seats when you sit near them because they don't want to catch any of the 'diseases that Africans are known to bring over here,' to having security called to follow you down the aisle in a department store in fear that your sticky fingers might steal something, and to more consequential incidents like being turned down for a lease application because the White landlord doesn't rent to your kind, to being charged extremely high interest rates for car, home, and furniture loans, to being stopped, questioned, searched, and detained by cops because you happen to be walking down the street in a White neighborhood while Black, and to being savagely attacked by a mob of White guys because you are seen hanging out with your White girlfriend or boyfriend, the life of a Black person is not easy down there. I laugh at myself often when I think about how I came here naively assuming that I would easily fit in and be accepted in America, the land of the free, especially in a predominantly Black area like the Delta. What I have personally experienced in the six months since I got to the United States has been horrendous."

"It's really harrowing! I go through it quite often myself, even in a metropolitan city like Memphis that has heterogeneous communities and numerous international corporations. For example, I had a middle-aged patient who was severely injured in a ghastly car accident some weeks ago, and he was airlifted to my emergency room. Can you believe that the man asked if there wasn't a White doctor available because he wasn't going to be touched by a nigger? This fellow's left leg, arm, and multiple ribs were fractured, and he was barely conscious due to the severity of his injuries and the amount of blood he had lost, but he suddenly had a burst of lucidity, just enough to express his preference for a White doctor. His wife and siblings who had arrived just as he was being rolled in didn't seem surprised about his stern desire and they did not object either. I told them that I was the only physician on call that night, and that they were welcome to take him to any of the other hospitals in the county or across Stateline in Mississippi, but that he wouldn't make it to any of them alive given his precarious condition. Before I even finished talking, he went into a coma, and only then did his family allow us to give him the care that he urgently needed."

"I hope he didn't survive because an evil person like that needs to rot in hell. Did he make it?"

"I'm damn good at what I do. I saved the moron's life, but I didn't get a 'thank you' from him or his family. My team and I treated him professionally throughout his stay in our hospital."

"That was remarkably nice of you. I must admit that since I arrived in the United States six months ago, there have been times, especially during the first few weeks, that I have wondered if I made the right decision accepting the job in Mississippi. As a Francophone who was born and bred in the Anglophone zone, I struggled my whole life to belong in either part of Cameroon. I was called names like 'Frog,' 'Anglofou,' 'Francofool,' 'Bamenda,' and 'Came no go,' depending on whether I was amongst Francophones or Anglophones. When I attended the University of Yaounde I in the mid to late nineties, I heard the slur 'Anglo-bami' that both English- and French-speaking individuals used to otherize people like me, to underscore a perceived dual allegiance, to highlight an implied superficiality of our roots, and to emphasize the slippery nature of trusting the subjects of this xenophobic slur. In the early nineties, when this mistrust almost led to the lynching of my family and me and to the burning of our home during an attack by an angry mob that was fed-up with the marginalization of Anglophones by the overwhelmingly Francophone government, I prayed for acceptance. I longed to be somewhere where I could fit in totally.

That only got worse over the years as the older I got, the more aware I became of the systemic injustices against Anglophones and the consequent growing mistrust of anything and anyone remotely linked to the French-speaking parts of the country. Thus, cultural mulattos like me, for lack of a better term, were constantly caught in the middle of the Anglophone versus Francophone conflict, and when I saw the opportunity to teach in the United States, I pounced upon it. I had learned in middle and high schools, from movies, books, magazines, and newspapers and from conversations with American Peace

Corps volunteers and from Cameroonians living in the United States that this country was the land of absolute liberty, equality, and freedom for everyone living in it. So, I left Cameroon, six months ago, convinced that I would be welcome, accepted, and allowed to fit in at my destination, but what I started witnessing upon arriving was absolutely chilling and shocking."

"So, have you been so disappointed that you have felt like you should have stayed in Cameroon?"

"Actually, I've weighed the pros and the cons of living in this country, and I've arrived at the conclusion that I'm better-off here. I've tremendous opportunities here that I couldn't even have imagined in Cameroon. Furthermore, the US is a nation of law and order, although occasionally, you hear about situations of gross injustice, but when sufficient light is shed on them and the evidence is presented in a court of law, the full force of the judicial system is brought to bear on the perpetrators in most cases, unlike in Cameroon where systemic corruption and widespread lawlessness allow for all kinds of atrocities to occur frequently with total impunity. Therefore, while I'm aware of my exposure to some really bad things in the United States because of the color of my skin and my immigrant status, I still believe that I'm better protected here than in my own home country, Cameroon."

"You're absolutely right, Joey. I feel the same way."

By that time, a couple who had returned to the chairs across from Joey and his interlocutor leaned forward and the lady asked, "Solange, is this your date?"

"No, this is Joey. It's his first time at CAMSUS. He's visiting from Indianola, MS where he's a teacher. Joey, meet Marie, an active member of our Cameroonian community in Memphis."

"Nice to meet you, Marie," Joey said while shaking the hand of the flamboyantly clad lady with heavy make-up.

"Great to meet you too," she responded. She held on to his hand longer than the average handshake, and that did not go unnoticed by the two onlookers.

Noticing Marie's companion's angry stare, Joey quickly extracted his hand just as Solange was saying, "Accompanying Marie tonight is her longtime boyfriend, Marcel."

"Oh yes, I'm sorry, Joey, please meet my boyfriend, Marcel," Marie said quickly, like someone who had been momentarily carried away by something but had suddenly regained her mind.

"It's a pleasure meeting you," Marcel said, extending his hand.

"Nice to meet you, bro," responded Joey as he shook hands with the jealous boyfriend.

Marcel was a short, shy fellow who seemed to have gotten used to being in his girl's shadow.

"So, how long have you lived in Indianola, handsome," Marie asked.

"Just six months."

"Do you like it down there? I hear it's like a third world country in the Mississippi Delta; is that true?"

"Yes, it has its flaws, just like any other place, but I'm making the best of it."

"I see; some members of this group have traveled down to that area for work and other reasons, and they have brought back stories of amazing food, of beautiful scenery, of warm people but also disturbing accounts of racism. Polycarp, the guy in the olive suit on the dance floor, for example, said last year that he stopped in Cleveland for lunch at a restaurant on Highway 61, and he was ignored for almost an hour, during which time other people, all of them White, trickled in one after another and were immediately seated and waited on. He said that he stood up to complain that he had arrived long before all the people that had been seated since he got there, but he was told by the manager that there was a Church's Chicken not too far down the road."

"That's not surprising as incidents like that abound in the Delta," said Joey. "Experiences like that are what Solange and

I were talking about when you and Marcel came," he continued. "It's terrible that people feel like they have to treat fellow human beings with such disdain and humiliation. I previously thought that it was something unique to Mississippi, but I just learned from Solange that big cities like Memphis are not any better."

"Absolutely not!" interjected Marcel. "Racism is everywhere in this country, more in some places than others. For instance, three years ago, I worked for a company specialized in medical research. I was their most credentialed and most experienced researcher, with a Ph.D. in biomedical engineering from Oxford and another doctorate in biochemistry from UCLA. By the time, I already had 24 articles published in internationally renowned medical and scientific journals, but when I submitted a proposal to the CEO for a significantly impactful and innovative project that would have revolutionized the way brain diseases are diagnosed, he did not seem interested in the idea. He said that he would run the idea by other executives in the company, but when, a month later, I sought an update for the third time, my other boss, the COO, chuckled and told me, 'That kind of proposal from a Black guy with a weird last name and a terrible accent like yours will never get anywhere in this company. What did you expect?' I'll never forget that meeting for as long as I live. That was certainly the worst day of my life; it felt like I had been stabbed right through my heart with a scepter."

"That's unbelievable!" Solange exclaimed, her face expressing utter disgust.

"Yes, that's some disgusting stuff," Joey added.

"What's even more sickening is the fact that they had secretly taken my proposal and replaced my name on it with the names of two White colleagues. When I found out about what they had done, I immediately resigned. The two individuals, a guy and a lady, struggled to execute the idea after my departure, and the CEO and COO called me repeatedly, initially to work as a consultant in order to get the project off the ground and running, but when I turned down that proposal, they tried what they thought was an offer I couldn't refuse: they offered me my job back with a 50% pay raise, but I told them to take everything and shove it deep up their you-know-what."

By that time, more people had regained their seats in the hallway where Joey was keenly listening to Marcel's story. Everyone burst out laughing at what he told his bosses.

"You know, what that COO said about your name reminds me of something that happened to a Tanzanian that I knew in Ohio," said Solange. "He had applied for a job at a prominent company in the state but had not heard anything about the status of his application for several months, until one day, after reading the story of a Nigerian who was the president of a college in Georgia, he decided to do something really drastic. The Nigerian he read about had applied for scores of jobs in all 50 states without success, but one day, he decided to drop his native African name in favor of a common Caucasian American one, and just like magic, he started getting the calls and job offers that he had been pursuing unsuccessfully for years, and he eventually went on to experience remarkable professional success in higher education institutions in this country. Thus, my Tanzanian friend gave that strategy a try, and he reapplied for the same position that he had previously applied for recently, with the same information as before, except for the Jewish name that he adopted. Guess what! Two hours after reapplying for the opening, he received an invitation via email to interview. They also called him six times within 24 hours and left voice messages. Although he could not go to the interview since the name change wasn't on his official documents, at least he got a consolatory closure as he found out that the scores of rejections had nothing to do with his academic qualifications or what he knew or what he was able to do; they were all based on his name which gave away his ethnicity and race."

"Yep, some incredibly crazy things are happening to Black immigrants in this county," one of the new arrivals, an older lady, chimed in. She got emotional while recounting a personal experience that happened very recently, just six days earlier.

"I'm a devout Christian, and going to church regularly on Sundays has been a tradition in my family since I was born. In my Baptist church, holding hands with other congregants while saying the lord's prayer is also customary, but there's this White lady at my church who always declines to hold my hand whenever I sit next to her, although she would enthusiastically hold the hand of any White person near her. I keep extending my hand to her, even as recently as last Sunday, hoping that Christ would touch her heart and she would look past the color of the hand and see a brethren made in God's image, like the Bible says."

"Racist people like her fill the pulpits in churches around this nation on Wednesdays and Sundays," her husband added. "In fact, it's common knowledge that 11:30 am on Sundays is the most racist hour of the entire week, because in communities around America, people flock to all White or all Black houses of worship or to heterogeneous churches, but still would hardly view one another as equals before God. If someone like us finds themselves in the wrong church on any given Sunday, they would get the kind of treatment that my wife just described. Not surprisingly then, it's said that some people interpret the 'Love thy neighbor as thyself' to mean the neighbor who looks like you."

"Some of the things that happen in God's house or that some people do in his name in this country would make you puke," his wife interrupted. Furthermore, she asked if anyone saw the report on CNN some months earlier about a couple in one southern city who categorically refused to lease their event hall to a biracial couple because their Christian faith did not endorse interracial marriage. "As I watched that on TV, I wondered what Christian faith they were referring to, but intentional and ignorant mischaracterizations of God and of biblical teachings are happening every day, and it's scary."

"Didn't slave traders and slave masters use entire chapters or verses in the Bible to justify their trading, ownership, and torture of Blacks for profit? Frederick Douglass wrote prolifically about slavery and the hypocrisy of its promoters. His autobiography aptly describes that, and everybody should read that beautiful masterpiece. It's called *The Narrative of the Life of Frederick Douglass, an American Slave.* He shows how racists misappropriate the Bible, the Church, and God for personal gain, to assert their superiority over other races, and to advance their agenda," another eavesdropper said very loudly that he drew the attention of even more people to the group that was getting too large for the narrow hallway.

"I've read it about 11 times; it's one of my favorite books. My husband likes it too," said the lady who talked about her encounter at her Baptist church. Joey found out later that her name was Susan and her husband's was Charles. She followed up with another account about her son's new school in Collierville when the 2008/2009 school year started.

"When we walked into his 6th grade classroom on the first day of school, his teacher looked at his name on his shirt and immediately asked him if he spoke English. That instantly took me to a very bad place, and before I knew it, I was asking this lady how else could my child have made it to the 6th grade if he didn't speak English. I was so mad that I called her out for profiling my child in front of other parents without any shame. Charly and I let the principal know about our discontent, and we urged him to have a talk with the teacher and perhaps his entire staff about racial profiling, bias, and diversity because we didn't want our son or any other child to be treated unfairly by anyone at that school because of where they came from or the color of their skin. I hardly ever lose my cool, but I think what happened that morning suddenly ignited a massive and explosive buildup of suppressed anger caused by personal traumatic experiences with racism, profiling, and xenophobia that I had endured, calmly and silently in America for two decades, and in an instant, boom, everything exploded!"

"That's understandable, Susan. Your maternal instincts kicked in instantly when you saw the White lady racially profile your child, and it reminded you of very painful personal experiences that you didn't want him to ever experience," someone chimed in.

"You're so right," Susan responded and then added, "Black immigrants in this country just go through so much racism and xenophobia on a daily basis, and most of the time, they can't or won't do anything about it."

"And sadly, sometimes encounters with racist individuals have led to the death of our brothers and sisters," another person in the group contributed.

"For instance, last year, my younger brother was driving down a street in a part of Oklahoma that he wasn't familiar with, and he ended up in a cul-de-sac in a White neighborhood. As he was trying to find his way out of there, he got cornered by a group of guys in pickup trucks flying American and confederate flags and bearing bumper stickers that promoted neo-Nazi and xenophobic ideas. They jumped out of their trucks and pulled him out of his car, and, just like that, started hitting him with anything they could use, including baseball bats, two by fours, brass knuckles, and metal pipes. They beat him to a pulp and left him for dead on that dead-end street and, just as suddenly as they had appeared out of nowhere, they quickly vanished into thin air. Hours later, my brother was found and taken to the hospital by some good Samaritans. The doctors and nurses tried their best to save his life. He was in the ICU in a coma for three months, and one day, he improved remarkably and was able to speak, however faintly. He told us how when his attackers noticed his African accent, they became more vicious and started snarling and growling like carnivorous predators in the jungle. They told him that he should have kept his stinky nigger ass in Africa with the rest of the monkeys, but, since he had chosen to bring his Black behind to their country, they would send him back to the animal kingdom in a pine box. His condition continued to improve slowly for about two months after regaining consciousness, and we were nourishing hope that he was really going to make it, but one night, his health took a sudden but rapid turn for the worse, and we lost him."

"Oh, my God! That's diabolical! Did they ever catch the monsters who did that to him?" Joey asked, visibly shaken.

"Nope, even though most of the homes in that neighborhood had security cameras, especially in the cove where it happened, and they certainly caught the entire incident on video. The police keep telling us that they are still investigating, that they have very little information other than what my brother was able to provide about the race of his killers, the type of cars they were driving, and the objects they used to beat him. Even after a year, they haven't found anything new about my brother's murder, but to tell you the truth, I believe that they know who those guys are, and they are just protecting them. Every time I have gone there to ask for an update on the case, I have left feeling that the murder of a Black immigrant by a group of racist White men would not feature among the top 1000 things on the to do list of that predominantly Caucasian police department. There is also the fact that no pressure is being put on them to look into my brother's murder. I am the only person in my family here in the United States, and I am just a student myself like my brother was. I don't have the means to get a lawyer to stay on this case, to give it the attention that it deserves. It's hard to not assume after a year of dealing with those cops that Black lives, especially the lives of Black immigrants, don't matter to them."

"But Black lives do matter, their feelings too," strongly emphasized Susan, attempting to console the speaker, Peter, who, at that point in his narrative, was sobbing and trembling and throwing his hands in the air in resignation. Moved by the gut-wrenching story, everyone surrounded Peter and told him to take heart, to be hopeful, to have faith in God, and to trust that he will provide justice for his brother.

Some people in the living room saw the circle that suddenly formed in the tight corridor and thought that a medical emergency had occurred, and they sprinted in that direction, and when they were told what was happening, they too wanted to get on the soapbox, and before long, the hallway could not hold that crowd anymore.

Joey could not believe what was happening. It looked like every one of the dozens of Cameroonians had at least one personal experience with racism and xenophobia in the United States.

In the same vein, one of the newcomers contributed to the talk by recounting what happened to him when he worked in Athens, GA, for one of the largest hotel chains in the world. At the time, his American colleagues often underestimated and downplayed his abilities, experience, and knowledge, and they frequently told him during meetings to be quiet because, "Africans are ignorant, primitive, and stupid and nobody wants to hear what they have to say because it's not worth shit over here." However, he kept his head down and ignored the abuse, insults, and slurs for several months while giving the job 100% of his energy and effort since he needed the income from it to feed his family. Unfortunately, the harder he worked, the more he was seen as a threat by his coworkers and the more frequently they continued throwing the "nigger," "monkey" and "Go back to Africa!" at him.

"Then one day," he continued, "I was told at a hastily called team meeting that my boss's missing wallet had been found among my belongings and his $900 was not in it. I told them that there was no way the man's wallet could be among my stuff because, one we don't share working space for me to have mistakenly picked up his wallet, and two, I don't steal. I let them know that I might be poor and miserable, but I was raised by God-fearing parents who taught me better. I implored them to go and pull the video from the security cameras, and they would find the real thief, if indeed the wallet was really stolen and not planted among my belongings in order to accuse me of stealing since 'Everybody knows that you all hate me in this place.' I was livid, and I spilled my guts out that evening. Can you believe they were even threatening to press charges on me? They told me that if I resigned, they would not get the cops involved, but I remained steadfast on getting the truth out as I knew I hadn't done what they were accusing me of, but when my boss refused to review the security footage or even conduct a basic investigation, I understood then that they just wanted me gone, so I left. Luckily for me and my family, the Lord blessed me with a significantly better job as the manager of another big hotel a week later."

A few loud "Amens" could be heard at the happy conclusion of the harrowing story, then another guy who was a high school science teacher added, "That's some messed up stuff right there!" He went on to say that the worst kind of racism is "intra-racial racism, if there is any such term, and if it doesn't exist, then it needs to be added to the dictionary, because the hatred of Black people by Whites is well-documented and often doesn't surprise anyone when it occurs, and therefore could be anticipated, but we Africans don't expect, don't ever anticipate that Black Americans would treat us the same way that White racists and xenophobes do, and that, my people, is best captured by the phrase intra-racial racism."

He substantiated by saying that "90% of the times that I've been told to go back to Africa or that Africans are usurping Americans' jobs has been by Blacks that I worked with or taught or met at professional development sessions or came across while out running errands. Additionally, White people hardly ever make fun of my accent, but it occurs quite frequently when I am with people who look like me. They tell me to 'drop that click-click language and speak American' like there's a language called American."

There was unanimous concurrence with what Fred, the teacher, had shared, and he proceeded to cite some insightfully significant statistics about racism in the United States as experienced by Black immigrants. "I recently came across a survey that was conducted earlier this year by one of our Cameroonian brothers, Dr. Michael Ticha, who is a professor in Texas and has written extensively about racism, nationalism, and xenophobia. According to him, 61.5 % of Black immigrants in this country have been victims of racism, while 38.5% of them haven't personally experienced it. Also, 51.9% of the individuals surveyed stated that they had been victims of what I called earlier intra-racial racism, whereas 48.1% of the Black immigrants in the study said that they had not been subjected to that kind of treatment. Therefore, most Black immigrants in America have or are experiencing what we have been talking about here tonight. The pressing question after we hear all these acutely distressing stories is what are the best ways to deal with situations of hate?"

Some suggested ignoring the fools who treat Black immigrants hatefully, walking away and letting God fight the battle, while others thought that reporting the problem to a supervisor or to the authorities, whenever possible, would be a better option, but the latter idea was mocked and criticized by those who thought that the approach could only lead to retaliation and retribution, which in some cases could be violent and even fatal. A few people preferred using instances of hate as teaching opportunities to educate the perpetrator about cultural, ethnic, and racial diversity, acceptance, and sensitivity, but this proposal provoked so much laughter and cynicism in the crowd, as it was viewed as tremendously naïve and weak.

The most popular remedy advanced was one that involved the victim of hate fighting back verbally or physically or both, if they could, as those in favor of the approach thought that it was incredibly important for any racist or xenophobic scum to be ridiculed and shamed on the spot, immediately. The hollowness of their brain needed to be revealed to them without delay. "When you stand your ground, they would know not to fuck with you anymore; excuse my French. They may not respect you after that; hell, they never did before, but I promise you, they would think twice before messing with you again," Fred concluded, to a thunderous applause and laughter from his audience.

Joey looked at his watch; it was 17 minutes to midnight. He couldn't believe that the group talk therapy session had gone on for more than three hours, and some people were not ready for it to end. Those who had not said a word wanted to share their own experiences with the crowd of their fellow countrymen and women. They did not want to return home one more time with the bubbling, corrosive memories that they had been carrying for a very long time, for some of them. They certainly considered the mass, whole-group discussion to be therapeutic.

Consequently, those who needed refills rushed into the house to get them and returned to the group in the backyard for some more heart-sinking personal accounts of encounters with racist and xenophobic individuals in the United States. Joey listened attentively until Sam emerged from the back door to look for him.

"Are you ready to go?" Sam asked.

"Whenever you're ready to leave, I'll be ready too," Joey responded.

"Awesome! Let me grab my keys and we can head out. I've to take my family to church in the morning."

On the way back to his house, Sam asked his guest what he thought about the CAMSUS meeting.

"It was so much fun. I ate so many different things that I hadn't eaten since I left Cameroon. I also met some nice people. I was very surprised to learn that all of them had heartbreaking experiences with racism in America, and that, strangely, made me feel better, because I realized that I wasn't alone. I really enjoyed myself tonight, and I'll definitely sign up to be an active member so that I can attend the monthly meetings."

"That's awesome! I'm glad you had fun and got a chance to meet so many of our members. It's stunning that, although we come from different backgrounds and are on individual journeys here in the United States, our experience with hate is one of the things that we all share, and it's very therapeutic just talking about it together and collectively brainstorming strategies to combat the evil."

"That's so true, but what's still confusing to me is the fact that, in a country that was founded by immigrants, some people feel like they have the right to tell others, who came here legally, and many have earned American citizenship, that they do not belong here."

"It makes no sense. Immigrants built this nation, and Black immigrants from all over the world, especially from Africa, are still contributing enormously to its development in all sectors of life. In fact, according to a recent study conducted by the Pew Research Center, compared to other demographic groups in the United States, foreign born Black immigrants are more likely to have a college or advanced degree, and, therefore, are more likely to have good jobs that translate into significant tax dollars for the government, tremendous flow of cash into the economy in terms of home, car, furniture, appliance, fashion, food, drinks, and other purchases. Therefore, we are a force to reckon with when it comes to the growth and the sustainability of this country, and I just wish that people would understand that and treat us with the respect and dignity that we deserve," Sam said passionately.

Joey thought about what his host said and then responded with the same passion, "There're thousands of foreigners living and working in Cameroon, including North and South Americans, Europeans, Asians, Australians, and citizens of other African countries. They are welcome with open arms in the communities where they live, and they are afforded even more significant protection by both the government and the citizens, than the natives. For example, can you imagine if a Cameroonian did anything nefarious to one of the thousands of Peace Corps volunteers who teach in urban and rural areas in Cameroon? All hell would break loose. The perpetrator or perpetrators would be caught by members of the community and, perhaps, lynched before the police arrive for tarnishing the reputation of the community nationally and internationally. We treat our foreign guests back home with tremendous respect, dignity, decency, and pride, regardless of their race, gender, ethnicity, etc. I recall how excited my family was whenever we had international guests at our house or foreign patrons at my mother's restaurant. We would bend over backwards to make them feel welcome, to make them feel at home. But, alas, we can't go a whole day here without being reminded by someone or a group of people that we don't belong here."

Sam eased the car into the garage right as his passenger was concluding his remark. It was almost 2 am.

Joey got back on the road to Indianola at 10 am after having breakfast with his hosts. He thanked them for their hospitality and generosity, and they told him that he was always welcome at their home. He too extended an invitation for them to visit him in Indianola whenever they wanted. On his way, he reflected on his brief stay in Memphis, how invigorating and refreshing it was. He was very thrilled by the new-found fun-filled getaway and relaxation opportunity that he had discovered, and he eagerly looked forward to his next visit to the Bluff City, hopefully with his sweetheart, Emily.

CHAPTER SEVEN

INDEPENDENCE DAY AT
THE GOLDMANS'

Joey's first full semester of teaching in the United States was very hectic but immensely productive, and, when it was over, he craved opportunities to take his mind off some of the disheartening things that he had experienced in so short a time. Therefore, for the second time in less than two weeks, he was traveling again for fun, heading to Bear, DE.

He drove to the Memphis International Airport early on July 3rd to catch a 9:05 am flight to Baltimore, MD where an eager and ecstatic Emily was waiting in the baggage claim area to drive him to her hometown.

I'm so happy to see you, JJ; I've missed you so, so, so much!" She said as she jumped into his widely open arms.

"I've missed you more, pretty," he responded softly after a prolonged kiss, still hugging her tightly.

"Did you have a good flight?"

"Yes, it was very smooth. It wasn't as long as I thought it would be."

On the way to Delaware, she wanted to know everything he had been doing since the last time they were together, even though she pretty much had been speaking to him multiple times daily since then. Thus, he gave her a narrative of his days without her, starting with the evening after the embarrassing encounter at the restaurant in Indianola. Then he told her about the days following that event, and when he got to the part about his visit to the Cameroonian community in Memphis, she got particularly inquisitive.

"Were there many ladies there?"

"Yes."

He hesitated before responding. His instincts warned him about booby traps in questions like that, especially when they were asked by a lover.

"Single ladies?" She threw more bait, but he was too smart for that. Besides, he had nothing to hide; he hadn't done anything wrong since she left with her parents.

"I don't know. I didn't ask them. That wasn't the purpose of my trip. Besides, it would be utterly disrespectful to you if I were checking out single ladies at events, don't you think so?" He attempted to turn the heat on her and stop the uncomfortable questioning before it got too far and led to an unnecessary squabble.

She blushed, then asked, "I know that there are usually bevies of beautiful and attractive single ladies who are hoping to catch the attention of guys at parties like that. There certainly were quite a few Cameroonian beauties there, ready to mingle, and I've heard that African men like to be with one of their own, a girl from back home, a purebred from the motherland"

She had gone too far, and he decided to let her know that.

"Stop that nonsense! I don't like where you're going with that baseless deductive reasoning. African men like ladies from Africa; therefore, I would prefer to be with a girl from there since I'm from that continent? You're starting to sound stupid, ridiculous, and insanely insecure, and I know that you're not any of these," he countered.

"But..."

"I said cut it off!"

"But..."

He didn't let her finish what she was trying to say.

"Honey, it's you I love. It's you I want to be with. I love you with all my heart, and I don't want you to ever nourish the idea that there is any woman out there that I desire more than you. And by the way, that crazy thing that you just said about African men is classic stereotyping, and it's a fallacy. If we followed that same logic, then we could also say the same thing about White men preferring to be with ladies from their race, which you and I know is a gross untruth. Pure love is pure love, period! It's color blind and knows no boundaries!" he concluded.

"I just wanted you to reassure me, JJ. I don't ever want to lose you, babe."

He reached for her right hand and held it up to his lips and planted a gentle kiss on the back of it and said reassuringly, "You've nothing to worry about, sweetheart."

They made it to the hotel a few minutes after 3 pm. Dinner at her parents' wasn't until 7 pm, so they had plenty of time to burn, and for two hopelessly-in-love individuals who hadn't seen each other for over two weeks, that was a lot of time to play with.

"That was the best lovemaking ever!" she whispered in his ear as she laid, naked, in his arms.

"Yes, it was," he responded, trying to catch his breath, with about 55 minutes left before they were expected at the Goldmans' for dinner.

They quickly took a shower together, got dressed, and left the hotel for the 15-minute drive to Emily's home.

Located at the end of a private paved road that had pine and oak trees on both sides, the Goldmans' residence was a huge compound that was made up of multiple magnificent structures. The main house, a white two-story, castle-like building had 6 bedrooms, 5 1/2 bathrooms, a library, an office, an entertainment wing with a movie theatre and a game room in addition to the living room, dining room and kitchen. The white ceilings were very tall and vaulted and bore beautiful chandeliers and receding lights that reflected extraordinarily on the white marble floors. All the bedrooms were on the second floor along with the office.

A stone walkway from the main house led to a guesthouse that had two bedrooms, 1 1/2 bathrooms, a kitchen, and a breakfast area. On the right side of the walkway separating the main house from the guesthouse was a lushly sodded and concrete area that had an impressive swimming pool, a spacious outdoor kitchen, and a long, shaded dining table with a 10-seat capacity. On the opposite side of the walkway, about 50 feet from the main house, there was another longer and wider pathway that led to a high-maintenance, pentagon-shaped pond with a couple of canoes floating on the glistening water. Chairs that matched the color of most of the structures on the Goldmans' impressive estate could be seen on each side of the pond.

Fifty feet farther from the pond was a large, white storage building that was linked to the aquatic wonder area by a concrete driveway. All kinds of maintenance and entertainment equipment were stored in the facility.

Mr. and Mrs. Goldman seemed delighted to have Joey at their residence.

"Make yourself at home, and I hope you're hungry," said the lady of the house with a kind of enthusiasm that got Joey suspicious for a moment due to Mrs. Goldman's behavior toward him the very first time they met. Nevertheless, his faith in God and his absolute trust in his girlfriend kept him at ease. First impressions last a long time, and it's difficult to erase them. It's also true that many people realize a mistake they have made and apologize for it and genuinely take steps to atone for the wrongdoing, but in order for the atonement to be effective, the victim would have to scrape the wrong from his or her memory. Joey was more than willing to forget the episode in Indianola to build a meaningful relationship with the parents of his girlfriend.

"Yes, ma'am, I'm hungry," he responded.

Dinner consisted of cobb salad as appetizer, steak and salmon accompanied with baked potatoes, asparagus for entrées, and assorted fruit and cheesecake for dessert. Red and white wines, champagne, bourbon, and whiskey flowed abundantly during the meal that had more than enough to feed twice as many people as there were at the majestic table, including Mr. and Mrs. Goldman, Emily, and Joey.

It wasn't a quiet dinner as, apart from inquiring about their guest's flight, how he got to the airport and where he left his car, the hosts, especially the lady of the house, were also curious about Cameroonian cuisine.

"Cameroonians eat a lot of vegetables and starchy food," Joey said.

"What are some vegetable-based dishes that you eat back home?"

"There is ndole, eru, njama njama, kok, and pumkin leaves, just to name these." The more he named, the more curious she became. She asked for specifics about each one, including the recipe, the sides, what they tasted like, and comparisons to American foods.

"What is your favorite Cameroonian food?" she asked.

"I love to eat eru and fufu, but ndole with the same side or with ripe plantains is my favorite dish," he responded with animation.

"Is that available here in the United States?" she inquired.

"Yes, I had some at an event in Memphis several days ago, and I was told that there were stores and restaurants in Maryland that sold various raw and cooked food from Cameroon respectively.

"Oh, great. Maryland is not far from here. Tom and I will check out some of those stores, and the next time you visit, we will definitely have some Cameroonian food for you," Mrs. Goldman offered enthusiastically.

"You don't have to do that, ma'am. I'm already over-whelmed by your remarkable hospitality and generosity. Eve-rything you made for dinner tonight is incredibly delicious and must have consumed your whole day to prepare. I love Amer-ican cuisine," he emphasized.

"I'm not wondering if you loved what I prepared tonight or not. I just like to try new things, different cuisines and drinks from around the world, and it'd be great to try some-thing new from our daughter's boyfriend's home country," she insisted. Then, getting emotional, she did something that Joey couldn't see coming.

"You know, JJ, can I too call you JJ...?"

"Absolutely, ma'am!"

"...Thank you! I've not been at peace with myself ever since I treated you horribly and despicably in Indianola. I'm not go-ing to say that that wasn't like me, because that would not be true, because for generations in my family, we were taught by our great grandparents, grandparents, and parents to hate Black people, to look at them as significantly inferior to us, to view them as animals, not humans, and, therefore not worthy of any consideration, regard, and respect. I'm a perfect prod-uct of that indoctrinated hate. It was instilled in us and has been growing, unhampered for centuries, but my daughter and you have inspired me to change. I know that deep rooted racism is not going to be turned off like a light bulb, but I am committed to doing whatever it takes to be aware, apprecia-tive, and respectful of racial and cultural diversity here in the United States and around the world. Please forgive me for what I did to you in Mississippi. That was profoundly stupid and ignorant of me, and I'm still embarrassed till this day."

Her emotional apology had everyone at the table teary-eyed, and she was shaking profusely as the last sentence came out of her mouth.

"I forgot about that incident and forgave you that same day. I went home and prayed about it and put the matter in

God's hands. I had to do that to be at peace with Him and myself. Additionally, it wouldn't be fair to Emily if I carried that nightmare in my heart all the time."

Mrs. Goldman stood up and asked for a hug. Joey gladly obliged, and her husband and daughter did not want to be left out. The group hug next to the dinner table was very beautiful and heartwarming.

The unexpected apology was tremendously comforting and relieving to Joey. The rejection by some and the repeated racist and xenophobic acts and comments by others, including from his girlfriend's mother had started to trigger self-doubt in his mind. On extremely bad days, such as when the landlord rejected his quest to rent his house for no reason other than his race, he would get depressed and would beat himself up. One day, he even wondered if there were some credence to the racists' and xenophobes' claim that Blacks were inferior and Africans were usurpers of Americans' jobs respectively. The thought of immigrants taking the jobs of unemployed, highly qualified, and helpless American citizens provoked a sense of guilt in him and made him feel like he had acquired what he had in America through the benevolence of someone. However, he shook off the dark contemplations as just the work of the devil trying to sow seeds of doubt in his mind at a vulnerable moment.

"That right there is the goal of the racists and the xenophobes, to torment their victims emotionally or physically to the point that it causes them to doubt themselves, to develop low self-esteem and self-worth, and to even question their identity," he would conclude, vowing not to ever let them win, not to ever give them the satisfaction that they sought.

But, unfortunately, the next wave of hate would be more severe than the previous one and would erode the vow to its core, and he would relapse into obscure ponderings again, even if just momentarily.

Therefore, the apology of one of the most vicious racists

he had met in his six months in America was a self-esteem and self-confidence and morale booster. It gave him hope and reassured him that he was worthy of everyone's respect and appreciation, including those of White people. He owed no one an apology for being Black nor for being an African immigrant with a teaching job. Yes, Tara Goldman's expression of regret for her racist statements toward him was liberating and reaffirming, he thought.

Joey and his hosts tarried at the dinner table long after they finished eating, until midnight. Tom gave the guest an outline of what to expect the next day at the Independence Day celebration. He said that about 100 close and extended family members and friends would be coming over to their mansion for the festivities. There would be an abundance of food and drinks, and the culminating feature of the event would be a spectacular fireworks show.

Joey asked if he could come over early in the morning to help with the preparations, but Tom declined his offer, saying, "Thanks for offering to help, JJ, but it won't be necessary. A catering service will be in charge of everything, including cooking, setup, serving, clean up, etc. Our staff here at the house will also be assisting. Just arrive ready to have a blast at your very first July 4th celebration in the United States."

"Thank you again for inviting me. I can't wait to see all the magnificent things that you have planned," Joey responded.

Mr. Goldman and his daughter took their guest back to his hotel at 12:15 am. Because it was so late, he did not want his daughter to be alone on the road, although the two lovers would certainly have preferred for him to stay at home and allow them another moment of privacy. They did not mind the dad's presence on the ride, though. There would be another opportunity for them to get together before Joey's return flight to Memphis, perhaps after the celebration.

"It was a pleasure having you at dinner tonight. Have a restful night, and see you tomorrow," Mr. Goldman said as he pulled up right at the entrance of the Comfort Suites.

"I had an amazing time tonight. Thank you so much for everything. Have a great night!" Joey responded and turned to his girlfriend who was sitting in the front passenger seat by her father and said, "Goodnight, babe. I love you!"

"I love you more. I will call you when I get home."

He waited for her call when he made it to his room, and it came as he was almost dozing off. They spoke for just a few minutes about the highlight of the dinner, her mom's remorse for her behavior weeks earlier. They both expressed optimism about the sincerity of the apology and the goals that her mother set for herself regarding racial diversity and understanding, and they both promised to support her in that regard.

They wished each other good night again and professed immense love for each other for the thousandth time that night, and then Joey went to sleep.

He had been sleeping for 10 straight hours when his cellphone rang at 11:00 am. Without looking at the caller ID, he answered, "Hello!"

"Hey babe, you're still sleeping?" Emily asked.

"Yes, I was, honey. What time is it?"

"It's 11 o'clock."

"Oh wow! I've been sleeping for 10 hours."

"Yes, you have. You're going to get up and get something for breakfast? I think the continental breakfast at that hotel closed at 10:30, but there's a good restaurant across the street."

"Okay, I'll do that."

"I would bring you breakfast, but I have to help my mom with something.

"That's okay, pretty. I'm not too hungry. I'll just get something very light."

"Yes, you don't need to eat a lot, because there will be all kinds of food in significant amounts here at the house very soon."

"Okay!"

"I'll pick you up at 4:30. Oh, one more thing before I forget: I know you like to wear a suit or, at least a sports coat to lunch and dinner invitations, but you don't need to wear any of those to this event. Dress casually, jeans and t-shirt; actually, many people will be in shorts and t-shirt, because we'll be outside, and it is supposed to be up to the nineties today."

"I'm glad you mentioned that, because I was going to wear my favorite pair of jeans and a sports coat over a button-down shirt.

"I know my man very well; that's why I thought I should inform you ahead of time. Okay, I got to go. I'll see you in a couple of hours. I love you!"

"I love you too, honey! I can't wait to see you later today."

Just as Tom Goldman had said, there were 100 to 105 guests at the event. Emily's maternal and paternal grandparents were there, as well as her uncles, aunts, and cousins from both sides of the family. Neighbors, friends, and colleagues of the hosts were not left out.

Food and drinks were strategically laid out in several stations in the beautiful yard. There was a section for all kinds of appetizers, another for a variety of entrées and a different one for anything an ingenious chef could think of as dessert. Regarding drinks, the hosts made sure that all best tastes and types were available for their guests. From sodas to beers to wines to whiskey and cocktails, every invitee could definitely find something they wanted on the drink menu.

The catering company had elegantly clad staff members at each station to help inform the guests' choices of food and drinks and to serve them, while, for those who didn't feel like returning to a particular spread for a refill, there were waiters circulating, ready to pour anyone their drink or fetch them another bite from the table.

Most of the guests ignored the seats, preferring to stand in small groups and in pairs to chat and mingle while enjoying all the delicacies provided by their extravagant, generous, and stylish hosts.

As soon as Emily and Joey arrived at 5:30 pm, long after the party had started, due to last minute delays caused by a traffic accident on her way to the hotel, Mr. Goldman yelled from one of the small groups on the lawn, "Glad you finally made it, Joey. Come on, let me introduce you to my parents."

"Mom, dad, this is Joey, Emily's boyfriend that you have already heard a lot about. Joey, meet my parents, Bill and Sally Goldman."

"It's a pleasure meeting you," Joey said as he shook hands with the elderly couple.

"Nice to meet you," Bill Goldman responded

Emily's paternal grandparents were in their late eighties, but they were still very strong and healthy. Just like their son, they had exceptional taste in fashion, but their reaction to meeting their granddaughter's boyfriend left the latter wondering if they were happy meeting him or not. They were not exactly cold toward him, but they were not warm either.

"My parents are both retired lawyers," Tom broke the uncomfortable silence after the handshakes.

"Awesome! What kind of law did you practice?" Joey asked the older Mr. Goldman.

"I was a corporate lawyer for a few of the top banks in the world, while my wife, Sally, practiced family law," he responded dryly, reluctantly, and without follow-up.

"Impressive, really impressive!" Joey complimented.

Another long and uneasy pause ensued, and noticing that his parents would appreciate the absence of the stranger, the junior Mr. Goldman walked Joey around to show him the various items that were on the menu.

Mrs. Goldman was helping an elderly couple choose items from the dessert table when her husband, daughter, and her boyfriend approached.

"Hey Grandma and Grandpa!" Emily greeted excitedly as

she rushed to hug them warmly.

"Who is this young man with you, Tom?" the elderly lady asked just as Emily was about to do the introductions.

"This is my boyfriend, Joey, whom I have been talking to you and Grandpa about."

Before she could finish her sentence, her mother turned to her boyfriend with palpable excitement.

"Hey JJ!" Mrs. Goldman greeted and hugged the special guest, and then introduced her parents, "JJ, these are my parents, Richard and Emily Schwarz."

"It's an immense honor to meet you," Joey said, reaching for a handshake with Mr. Schwarz, but he did not reciprocate.

"What did I tell you, Dad?" Mrs. Goldman asked, furious and noticeably embarrassed, a reaction that was mirrored by her husband and daughter.

"Grandad and Grandma, I already told you that Joey was Black and how much I loved him. If you're not pleased to see him, that means you're not happy to see me either, and I'd rather not be around you if that's the case," Emily said, fighting back tears.

"Dad, Mom, you both will have to let go of these ridiculous beliefs and so-called family values that you proudly talk about all the time, because they make you look really stupid and ignorant. They prevent you from seeing the world the way it actually is and from appreciating and respecting other people like the bible that you speak of ceaselessly teaches, simply because of the color of their skin. As the proud Christians and church elders that you both are, you have to practice exactly what the good book says, and not discriminate against people who don't look like you, like us. I don't believe anymore in that blind and foolish heritage that you all speak of all the time, which you fight so obstinately to preserve and protect. The world has changed, and it's still changing drastically every day, and you all are being left behind. Can't you see that you're making your granddaughter unhappy?" Mrs. Goldman appealed, visibly hurt by what her parents had done.

Joey was very proud of her, as he realized that Mrs. Goldman was honest when she promised to change the night before. He pulled out a handkerchief from his pocket and handed it to her to dry the tears that were rolling down her cheeks. Two phenomenal White women and a White man were defending his right to be at the gathering, to date a family member, and it was an incredibly uplifting moment for the African.

The persons she was speaking to didn't seem moved by her emotional speech. They looked at her stone-faced, with palpable disappointment and disgust.

"Come on, Joey; let me show you the variety of food and drinks that we have," Mr. Goldman intervened, trying to change the subject and to extract the victim of the reprehensible behavior of his in-laws out of the uncomfortable situation that was drawing the attention of nearby guests. Emily left with them, arm in arm with her boyfriend.

"I apologize for that, Joey. All four of Emily's grandparents are stuck in their ways, but don't let that bother you," the host said, and then added, "I want you to enjoy yourself this evening. If there's anything you need that's not available here, just find me, and I'll see what I could do to get it for you. But, again, try to ignore the abhorrent and ignominious behavior of our parents."

"Thank you, sir; thank you very much!"

Joey and Emily sat down to eat at one of the tables in the shaded area near the swimming pool. He had a salad as an appetizer and BBQ spareribs, grilled chicken thighs, coleslaw and potato salad as entrées. To accompany all that food, he requested a bottle of water and something strong, a Manhattan, recommended by one of the servers. Emily had the same food items on her plate, but she opted for a strawberry margarita as her drink.

The ambiance at the event was fascinating to Joey. There were many kids and teenagers swimming in the pool while others were running around trying to splash water on one another with water guns. Several adults could be seen playing ping-pong, pool, poker, basketball, and other games that he had never seen. For instance, there was one where a person would sit in an elevated seat that was above a huge container filled with water, and another person would try to make him or her fall into the water by aiming a ball at a target that was just above the chair.

"What's that called?" Joey asked Emily.

"That is a collapsible dunk tank; do you want to try it? You may need a change of clothes though," she responded.

"They seem to be having a lot of fun. I may try it some other time. And what is that game that seems to be drawing a lot of attention too in front of the guesthouse?"

Emily looked over where Joey was pointing, and there was a group of guys and ladies aiming some objects that looked like pouches at a round hole on a large inclined, rectangular, boxlike object that had the stars and stripes of the American flag painted on it. The game seemed very popular among the guests, judging from the crowd participating in it.

"That's a cornhole game," Emily responded and added, "I'm actually an expert in it. I don't think there's anyone here who could beat me at the cornhole."

"When we get a chance, I'd like you to teach me how to play."

"Sure thing!"

When they finished eating, Joey wanted to try his hand at the table tennis. He had played it most of his teenage and adult years in Cameroon, but he hadn't had the opportunity to play since he arrived in the United States.

"Can you play?" Emily asked.

"I'll let you find that out shortly," he teased, smiling.

Her cousin, Mitch, a senior at Columbia University, had beaten everyone at the game since they started playing more than three hours earlier, and his numerous victories had gone to his head. He was bragging and trash talking, and when Joey asked to play, he responded, "Are you asking to play with one of the kids, because I'm sure you don't want me to humiliate you in front of my cousin."

Joey smiled.

"I tell you what: I'll play you with my left hand, to give you a chance; that way I don't beat you too badly. What do you say?" Mitch asked condescendingly.

"Whatever you want to do works for me. I just want to see if I can play," Joey pretended.

"Do you need to warm up?" Mitch asked.

"No, I don't."

As promised, Mitch served the ball with his left hand. It was such a brilliant serve that Joey easily missed as he tried to hit the ball. Mitch burst out laughing and asked mockingly, "Are you sure you want to do this? You're not even a match for my left hand."

His opponent did not respond, implying that he was willing to stay in the game. Thus, Mitch sent another impressive serve over the net and, although Joey was able to hit the extremely fast ball, it hit the net and came right back.

"2-0! Look, man, I don't want to disgrace you in front of your girlfriend," Mitch said arrogantly, but, just like before, Joey ignored him. He had better luck with the third serve, but after a back and forth that went on for over a minute, his last strike swooshed over the net, but didn't touch his opponent's side of the table, thus earning the latter another point.

By that time, it was clear to the spectators that the African was definitely not playing ping-pong for the first time. Two more serves by Mitch brought the score to 5-0, thus causing another round of trash-talking and boasting.

"Because you're the only non-white person at this celebration, I'm going to go easy on you," Mitch announced.

"I didn't notice that I was the only one, but thank you for mentioning that, and no, I don't need you to cut me any slack."

It was Joey's turn to serve. He missed three in a row, but, on the fourth one, he spun the ball so mesmerizingly that it caressed the net, landed on the other side of the table, and swiftly spun off the table, all at the speed of light. He had also noticed that his opponent struggled with balls that went to his right, so, he fired his next serve there as well, thus bringing the score to 8-2. With Mitch's Achilles' heel discovered, Joey hammered the ball to the right side of his opponent each time the latter served, five times in a row, to the amazement and applause of the spectators who were ecstatic to see someone threaten Mitch's lunch. Only one point separated the two players, and it was Joey's turn to serve once more. Everyone watching understood what that meant, and without surprise to anyone, even the trash-talking and bragging stopped.

Joey spun the serve beautifully. Mitch hit it back with an impressive fast spin. Joey replicated his opponent's move, and both of them went back and forth aggressively for a while until the Cameroonian lost. If Mitch got the next two points, he would win, but Joey was determined to not let that happen.

An idea from a distant past crossed his mind. One of his coaches had taught him to spin his serves with the back of his bat when he was 14, and that had helped him win many games back then. It could come in handy in defeating Mitch. Thus, he threw the white ball high up in the air, and, with a backhanded cut, he sent the ball spinning over the net with such force that it touched Mitch's side of the table and spun off to the turf before he could even realize what had happened. It was simply magical. Mitch was speechless. Joey did it again and again, and the spectators went wild. He was ahead by one point with victory just a point away.

"Are you okay, Mitch? Are you sure you want to continue with your left hand?" Joey asked sarcastically.

The ball went up in the air again. Same mesmerizing maneuver by the server, and it spun over the net and slid off the table. Mitch was motionless and in absolute disbelief. He had lost. Joey had come from very far behind and given him his first loss in more than three hours.

He asked for another round. He tried to blame his loss on his playing with his left hand, and he was not going to take any more chances the next time.

Joey quickly drank the rest of his cocktail that Emily was holding for him and sent her to get a refill while he returned to the table. All the cousins and family friends, all of them victims of Mitch's merciless hand at the table were on Joey's side for the ultimate showdown. They were cheering him and rooting for him, seeking to get their revenge through him.

Joey was first to serve, and the ball returned right back, at lightning speed. It was too fast for him. The next three serves were not different. Mitch was up by four points, but he blundered when Joey's last serve landed in front of him. When he hit the ball back, the net caught it. 4-1 was the score at the switching of service, as Joey was trying to figure out if Mitch had the same weakness when he was playing with his good hand. Additionally, he did not use the trick that had carried him to victory in the first game.

Ping came the serve, and he hit it right back. Mitch gave it a back hand, and the ball bounced so high on Joey's right, thus setting up an easy strike.

"4-2!" screamed one of the spectators. The next three serves revealed Mitch's weakness. He didn't do well with balls that landed on his left. Joey capitalized on that, thus getting ahead of his opponent by one point. The crowd was ecstatic. At that point. Mitch started showing signs of nervousness, and he began to fumble. That cost him the next point.

"6-4!" Emily shouted jubilantly and proudly.

It was Joey's turn to serve once more, and without surprise to the excited onlookers, he unleashed his magic trick successfully four times in row, thus putting Mitch one point away from the ultimate ridicule and shame.

"10-4!" screamed a voice that was very familiar to Joey.

It started raining taunts, jeers, and heckling from the jubilant spectators who were thrilled to see Mitch finally go down in shame.

Taunts and heckling have a way of demoralizing and frustrating any adversary who lacks confidence in himself, and Mitch seemed to have lost all of the confidence and pride that he had at the beginning of the first match with Joey. All the wind he had gained under his wings from three hours of endless victories was gone. He was conspicuously angry and frustrated.

It was his turn to serve, and when he hit the ball, it was caught by the net and returned to him.

That only meant one thing, and everybody knew it. Joey was swiftly swept off his feet and carried in the air like a trophy by the rejoicing spectators who were so loud that everyone at the party could hear them. He reluctantly allowed them to carry him around for about seven minutes, then he told them he needed to use the restroom.

"Why didn't you tell me that you were such an amazing ping-pong player? I could have asked you to teach me so that we could play together," Emily teased.

"I've been playing my whole life. I just never had the opportunity to play since arriving in the United States, but I'm going to teach you as soon as possible so that we can play together," he responded as they walked into the guest house for him to use the restroom.

When Joey came out of the restroom, Emily wasn't waiting for him in the breakfast area like she said. He wondered where she might have gone, but he assumed that she might not be far, perhaps in one of the rooms; so, he called, "Babe!"

No answer.

"Honey!"

Still no response.

"Emily!" he called, louder, but all he heard back was his own voice echoing through the guest house, then, suddenly, someone came out of the bedroom across from the bathroom. It wasn't Emily. It was a face he had seen upon arriving at the celebration earlier that evening.

"I sent Emily to get my medication from my wife. She'll be right back. I ate some sausage about an hour ago, and it raised my blood pressure. So, I came in here to lie down for a minute, but I forgot to retrieve my medication from my wife's purse."

"Oh, okay! I hope you feel better soon, Mr. Goldman."

"Thank you!" he responded, and then added, "You know, I've been hoping to speak with you at some point."

"Sure! About what, sir?"

"I don't mean to be disrespectful or racist or anything, but I think you're just trying to use my granddaughter to get papers to stay in my country like your folks come over here and do all the time, but I'm not going to stand by and let you tarnish my family's heritage and values that we have fought hard to preserve for many generations. I am not going to let you defile our beliefs and customs like that."

Joey was not surprised as he had heard rhetoric like that many times in the past few months, but he pretended he did not know what the old man was talking about.

"What are you talking about, Mr. Goldman?"

"You think I don't know about your little plans to take advantage of my granddaughter to stay in America? Everybody knows what you're trying to do! I tell you what; I can make you an offer that would get you your papers and keep my family's heritage and reputation intact, and I am willing to do this just because I love my Emmy with all my heart. She's our favorite grandchild, and for her to be with you, I assume she must have seen an element of decency in you; therefore, I've considered that too in my decision to make you this offer. I have a close family friend who's one of the most successful immigration attorneys in the entire United States, and he has powerful connections in the USCIS. He is at this July 4th party, and I can get him to obtain your papers for you very easily. I will take care of his fees and all the administrative charges, so you will not have to spend a dime! As a matter of fact, I could even throw in something for you, to help you settle down comfortably in America after you obtain your papers. What do you say, young man?"

"I say you're full of shit, old man; you're crazy!"

Emily heard Joey cussing angrily as she walked into the guesthouse.

"I'm not sure from where you got the idea that I'm with your granddaughter simply because I'm hoping to use her to get papers to stay in the United States, but that's insane! Only a lunatic could come up with a thought that ridiculous. For your information, Emily and I are together because we genuinely love each other profoundly. I don't know what the future holds for us, but I can tell you that the bond between us is iron-clad and unbreakable, at least it will not be broken by dumb, racist views and beliefs like the ones your family has proudly and blindly espoused for centuries."

"What's going on JJ?" Emily inquired, stunned by what she had walked into.

"Your exceptionally loving and protective grandfather here believes that I'm trying to use you to get papers to stay in the United States. He also thinks that my relationship with you has tarnished your family's heritage and customs, something he's not going to allow to continue; so he's making me an offer that he believes I can't refuse: he's going to get a powerful lawyer to get my papers to stay in America, and he is going to write me a check to settle anywhere I want in this country, on condition that I break up with you and never contact you again."

"What! Did you tell him that? How dare you, Grandpa? How dare you? You're nothing but a racist, disgusting pig. I can't understand how you can still be this hateful and xenophobic after attending Harvard and Cambridge and having a very successful law career that took you to more than a hundred countries. Based on your life trajectory and experience, you're supposed to be one of the most diversity-friendly people in this family, but somehow you've managed to hold on tightly to your racist, xenophobic roots."

"I'm just trying to protect my family, to protect our name, honey," Mr. Goldman said obstinately.

"What name? What heritage?" she yelled, tears streaming down her cheeks as she got in his face aggressively, almost knocking the old man off balance.

"You just don't like Black people, but, news flash, you can't impose your ignorant beliefs and values on everyone in this family!" She turned to Joey, and, taking his hand, she said defiantly, "Let's go, babe!"

"Just so you know, Mr. Goldman, I have a work visa to stay in the United States, and it's renewable, meaning that I can stay for as long I want. Maybe your immigration lawyer friend can explain to you how that works," Joey said gleefully on his way out.

Everyone was starting to gather around the pond for the fireworks show. Joey and Emily, still talking about what had transpired in the guesthouse, looked for a good spot to stand and watch the show. They settled for a space near her parents who had been wondering about their whereabouts.

"Where have you been? I've been looking for you. I even called your phone," Mr. Goldman said to his daughter.

"I was running an errand for Grandpa. He needed me to get his blood pressure medicine from Grandma and bring to him in the guesthouse."

"Oh, okay. He said that he was going to lie down for a minute, but he needed us to wake him up when the fireworks started."

"You won't believe what happened when I took the pills back to him; I walked in on him trying to bribe JJ to break up with me."

Emily and Joey gave her parents a full account of what happened in the guesthouse, and, while Mr. and Mrs. Goldman were not particularly surprised about the patriarch's behavior, they said that they were going to talk to him, again.

The show was everything that the extravagant host had

promised Joey it would be: fascinating and spectacular. Joey had never seen fireworks up-close. His only memory of them was seeing them on TV during New Year's Eve shows back in Cameroon. Being present at an actual fireworks show was thrilling to him. He thought that the bangs were significantly louder than on TV, but all the explosions made the show extraordinarily exciting to him.

The guests were snacking, drinking, dancing, chatting, and screaming joyfully as the fireworks were lighting up the sky colorfully with each explosion. The extravagance of the last phase of the Goldmans' July 4th celebration was truly spectacular.

The festivities ended later than planned, at 1 am, because the guests didn't want to leave, especially as there was still a ton of food and drinks left. Tom Goldman literally had to start dismissing the guests one by one for them to leave his property.

When everyone was gone, he and his daughter took their special guest back to his hotel.

Joey spent the next two days touring Washington, DC, Maryland, and Pennsylvania with his girlfriend before returning to Indianola. On the flight back home, he thought about how incredibly stronger the trip had made his relationship with Emily. Her grandparents' opposition to their relationship had only made them more committed to staying together, and for the first time since they started dating, he began to think about the what ifs of a forever life with her.

CHAPTER EIGHT

GROWING IN THE DELTA

Joey spent the rest of that summer resting and preparing for what was promising to be an incredibly busy school year as, not only would he be teaching full-time, but he would also be taking nine credit hours towards his doctorate. He broke the news about his pursuit of a doctoral degree to Emily the week before school started, and she was immensely encouraging and supportive. She also confirmed to him something that she had mentioned before when they had started dating.

"I think I've made up my mind about what I would like to do when my TFA three-year contract ends at the end of the upcoming school year."

"Really! Medical school or law school?"

"Law school; because of the appalling treatment that I have witnessed you go through, coupled with that I already was seeing happen to Black people, especially in the South, I would like to become a civil rights and immigration attorney to fight for the protection of the rights of victims of hate and xenophobia. I'll start studying to take the LSAT in January so that I can apply to law schools in the Spring. My grandfather and uncles have said that they'll help me."

The nobility of her decision and the rationale behind it endeared her in his mind even more. She had stood up to her parents in his defense when her mother had treated him with utter disdain and disrespect, and she was ready to abandon them in a restaurant thousands of miles away from their home. In addition to that, she had called out her grandfather's racism and threatened to walk out of his life when he had attempted to bribe Joey to break up with her. As if these acts of love were not enough, she was letting her love for him inspire her choice of a life-long career. That was tremendously heart-warming; it was monumental, he thought.

"What if I disappointed her?" he wondered. "Then she would spend a lifetime doing a job that she got into out of love for a man who broke her heart. That would be terrible, and I can't let that happen," he went on.

He decided that day that he was going to do his utmost best to deserve all the immense love and trust she had for him.

"Every sane man would be honored to have such a fiercely loyal partner and lover like Emily by his side," he concluded.

"That's an exceptional choice, babe, and I'm so proud of you for choosing that route. I'm going to fully support you every step of the way!" Joey responded to the news about Emily's decision.

"Thanks, JJ; that means a lot, coming from you."

Thus, Joey's second year of teaching in Mississippi and Emily's last started with a lot of anticipation. He had a brand-new group of students, and that meant going over routines, expectations, and procedures the first week of school. The students were very excited to take his class because of all the great things that his former students had told them about him. According to some of his new students, they were told that, "...his classes were appropriately rigorous, very well-structured and quite fun." Those who took his classes the prior year also reported that he was highly knowledgeable and was always looking for new ideas to enhance teaching and learning. They nicknamed him the "renaissance man."

Unfortunately, Joey discovered early that academic year that the arrival of a new group of students also meant the return of the all too familiar ignorant and stupid ideas and behaviors about Africans and immigrants. He did not mind answering their questions about where he was from, the types of food in Cameroon, what teenagers did on their free time, and other genuine inquiries, but, just like the previous year, a few students mocked his accent and made clicking sounds and yelled, "Buyaka Buyaka" and "Awawa Awawa" when they thought he was not watching.

However, unlike the previous year when, on the advice of his roommates, he would stop teaching and demand that the perpetrators of such blatant acts of disrespect own up to their offense or for the class to identify them, without any success, even when he would threaten to write up the whole class, he acted as if he did not hear the sounds and comments or as if he did not care about them with his new students. Surprisingly, the individuals who were advertising their ignorance in the classroom got tired of him not paying them any attention, and, after a few days, they stopped the nonsense altogether. Additionally, they were not helped by the fact that he would lower his voice and increase the speed of his speech whenever any foolishness irrupted in the classroom, and whenever he did that, most of the students would yell in unison, "Stop that nonsense; some of us are trying to learn!"

One would expect kids who were unhappy with their peers for disrupting an important lesson to report the culprits so that they could be appropriately disciplined, but, no, Joey's students were not that righteous. They might get very upset at their peers for disrupting class, but they would not snitch on them for any reason. Such cowardly loyalty was befuddling to their teacher.

As a proactive measure to promote international awareness and to curtail the type of questions and comments that he had become accustomed to, he introduced a weekly current event and reflection assignment in all six of his classes. Each of his 185 students was assigned a different country. The students in his French classes were limited to nations in the francophone world, while his English students could pick from any continent, but he ensured that every country in Africa was among the 185.

Essential tasks in the weekly assignment included finding a news article about a major event that occurred in the country during the week the assignment was due or, at least, the week before, effectively summarizing the article, and writing a reflection about the event. The reflection involved the students' thoughts and feelings about the event. For the first assignment, he required that students also research and present basic facts about their adopted country, including location, population, official language(s), government, economy, education, religion, sports and recreation, cuisines, and any other information that students deemed important. Every week, the news article had to be attached to the summary and reflection and submitted on Monday, and 10 minutes of each period was dedicated to discussing the students' findings.

The current event assignment was immediately impactful, as the students displayed overwhelming interest in discussing what they found out about their respective countries. Their curiosity about world affairs grew impressively, and, by the end of the first month of doing the assignment, the students were suggesting ways to expand and enhance the tasks. For instance, some wanted to bring food from their countries to class, while others wanted to dress up in native regalia from their nations on the due dates of the assignment. The most ambitious ones wanted to organize two international fairs: one at the end of the first semester, and another at the end of the school year. Furthermore, the students with African and Caribbean countries as well as Jamaica, Haiti, Guyana, Barbados, Trinidad and Tobago, and Granada were particularly interested in putting together a special show for the annual Black History program at the school.

All the brilliant ideas were taken into consideration, and, with the collaboration of the administration, the staff, and the parents, a beautiful celebration of Black history was done in February, while a spectacular international culture fair rounded off the very productive and successful school year.

Another highlight of that school year, an incredibly revealing and refreshing one for that matter, was the volunteer work that Joey did with the first-grade class at Carver Elementary. At the suggestion of the school district superintendent and with the agreement of his principal, he accepted to spend his planning period teaching French to first graders on Wednesdays and Fridays.

The students were highly engaged and excited on the first day that he taught them. They learned to say and sing the alphabet in French, and when he returned on Friday, every single one of the 33 kids from diverse backgrounds still remembered everything they had learned two days earlier. That was quite impressive, as he had not had that kind of experience since he started teaching French in the United States. When he taught them numbers and simple addition, subtraction and multiplication, they understood and retained everything a lot faster than the high school students.

By the second week, he was receiving thank you emails and phone calls from parents who were reporting that their son or daughter couldn't stop singing and teaching them numbers and alphabet in French and saying simple expressions like "Bonjour!" "Comment allez-vous?" "Je vais bien, merci."

Apart from noticing the exceptional retention levels of the elementary school students, Joey was also surprised that one month into the experience, no kid had asked him where he was from, nor did any of them comment about his accent. They were just thrilled by the opportunity to learn a foreign language. The only people who asked about his accent and where he was from were the faculty and staff of Carver as well as the parents who were able meet him. He wondered why none of the kids were asking him the types of stupid and xenophobic questions that he was getting from the high school students and adults. Were they just smarter than the high schoolers? Were they unaware of the fundamental thing that set him apart from any adults that they knew: his accent? After pondering these questions extensively and discussing them with his girlfriend, he concluded that hate and xenophobia were learned. The kids' minds were innocent, uncorrupted, and pure. That was why all they cared about was learning something new in a foreign language each time Joey arrived.

Minutes before his arrival, they would bunch up at the glass windows in anticipation, hoping to catch a glimpse of him as he was getting out of his car and walking towards the classroom. As soon as they saw him, they would start jumping with excitement and would run to open the door for him, while yelling, "Bonjour Monsieur Jumessi!"

He was running a few minutes late one Wednesday, and the elementary school principal called to say that the kids were already catching a major fit and some of them were crying. When he finally showed up, it was the most exciting thing he had ever seen. The children were so jubilant that one would have thought that they had just been told that they were going on a trip to Disney World. A couple of them stormed out of the classroom before their teacher and her aid could catch them and ran towards him, like kids who had not seen their father in several months. By the end of the school year, the students had learned so much that the superintendent invited their class to a school board meeting to show off some of their French skills.

Meanwhile, as far as his pursuit of a doctorate was concerned, strategic and creative thinking helped him navigate the challenges involved in attending classes at Delta State University on weekday evenings and on Saturdays. There was always an assignment due. The workload was so overwhelming that, at times, he thought about quitting, but the support and encouragement of Emily and his family spurred him on.

He found the individual assignments a lot easier to do than the group projects, because his classmates, most of whom were teachers and school administrators, allowed their ignorance and preconceived ideas about Africans to create a barrier between them and him, as they were unwilling to include him in their groups whenever a professor told the class to form groups, usually of four or five students. Sometimes, when the teacher would inquire why he was not being picked by any of the groups, Joey would hear excuses like, "We live too far away from him, and it would be difficult to get together to do the assignment," but when he would offer to meet them wherever they wanted him to come, they would say that their groups were already full.

Since he was not interested in begging anyone to work with him and the teachers were not compelling any groups to work with him, he would ask the professors if he could work individually, and they would grant his wish most of the time. Without surprise, he would do exceptionally well in the group assignments that he completed alone, and his brilliance was quickly noticed by everyone. Midway into the first semester, there was growing desire among his peers to work with him, but the hypocrisy and dishonesty in their requests were too conspicuous to not notice.

During lunch break one Saturday, a classmate of his who was a high school social studies teacher verbalized the real reason why people did their best to keep him out of their respective groups initially.

"They didn't want to catch any of the HIV and Ebola that y'all Africans bring over here, but I swear to God I wasn't one of them."

"I see; I'll make sure to continue keeping my distance in order not to infect anyone," he said sarcastically.

The fellow teacher, whose name was Patrick, continued his quest for rapprochement with Joey by further betraying the words and thoughts of their peers. According to him, "People didn't want your strong foreign accent to cause them to lose points during class presentations, but when you made that A+ in the curriculum evaluation project and another one in the introduction to educational leadership assignment, people were like, damn! This dude is very smart! And then, last week when Dr. Rushing applauded your work and used it as an exemplar, folks got together after class and started talking about getting you in their group for the next projects."

Joey thanked Patrick for disclosing what was being said about him behind his back, but he declined the offer to join the social studies teacher's group for the leadership theory and application project that was being assigned that day, and the professor needed the names of group members submitted before the end of class.

Nevertheless, on the first day of school for the second semester, a new classmate who was taking his first doctoral level course asked if he could work with Joey, and he accepted. The new student, Kevin, introduced him to two other classmates that Joey had never seen, and together, they formed the most successful group for the entire semester.

Globally, Joey's first year in the doctoral program was productive and as successful as his second year of teaching.

The last day of the school year at Gentry was bittersweet for both Joey and Emily as, while they were happy to have made it to the end of a particularly hectic academic year during which they had both taught full-time and still managed to pass all courses in graduate school and the LSAT respectively, they were forced to come to terms with the fact that they would not be able to see each other on a daily basis anymore since she was putting down the chalk permanently and heading to law school. Consequently, Joey threw a party in her honor and invited her close friends, TFA members in the Delta and a few colleagues. He also invited her parents, but they were not able to make it due to a prior commitment.

Halfway into the celebration, he asked for everyone's attention and, while fighting back tears, he gave an emotional speech in which he professed his immense love for his girlfriend of almost two years, and he expressed how much he would miss her, even though she had intentionally chosen the Cecil C. Humphreys School of Law at the University of Memphis to be close to him. He also left everyone guessing what exactly he meant when he concluded his speech with, "This is just the end of a chapter in a beautiful and enthralling story, a journey that's barely beginning."

CHAPTER NINE

GOING HOME

In the spring of 2012, Joey decided that it was the right time to take home the girl that his parents and siblings had heard him say so many great things about during the four years that they had been together. So, he called his father. After the usual greetings and asking about everyone in the immediate and extended family, even the family goats, pigs, chicken, dogs, and other animals, as is typical among Africans, he got to the main reason for his call. "Papa, I will be coming home in May."

Since he left Cameroon in December of 2009, he had not been back, to the chagrin of his parents and siblings who longed to have him around, even just for a few days, at least for Christmas, an important event that they had always celebrated together as a family since he was born.

The news of his upcoming trip to Cameroon was too exciting for his father to bear, and, after pausing for so long that his son got worried about what may have happened to him, he let out a very emotional, "Finally! That's the best news I've received in a very long time. You know, dealing with this diabetes and high blood pressure at my age, I don't get a lot of great days, but this is going to be an awesome one. Thank you, Jesus! I've been wondering if I'm ever going to see you again because of my health condition, but you've given me hope that that day is coming very soon. Do you know when exactly you'll be coming?"

"I'll be done with school on May 23rd; so, I'm thinking I could leave the United States two days later."

"Oh, wow! That's exactly one month from today. Your mother is going to collapse with joy when she hears about this. I'll be on my way home in a few minutes to break the news to her."

"I know; she's been telling me to come home all the time. I have just been having a lot going on. Teaching full-time and attending graduate school in America is not easy at all. Anyway, there's one more thing I need to tell you."

"What's it? Is everything okay?"

"Oh, yes, everything is great! I just wanted to let you know that I'll not be coming home alone. Emily will be with me. We've been together for four years now, and you already know how I feel about her; so, I think it's way past the time for her to meet my family and to see where I was born and raised. I have already met her family many times since we started dating; so, to better understand me, she needs to see the environment I came from and the people who shaped who I am today."

"That's fantastic! I'm so happy we'll get to meet her finally. I can't believe this, JJ! Your mother and I will start preparing the compound to receive our special guest. How long will you be staying in Mbengwi?"

"One month, but we'll travel a little bit during that time so that she can see Cameroon."

"That's great. So, let me ask you this then: what do her parents think about her coming to Cameroon? I remember you told me that her parents and grandparents did not like Black people, and that they did not approve of your relationship with their daughter."

"Well, her grandparents are still stuck in their old ways, but her parents have made significant progress and have become very supportive and encouraging of us. In fact, they too would like to visit Cameroon someday."

"Amen, to God be the Glory! We'll be glad to welcome

them too with open arms and hearts whenever they come."

His father talked for the rest of the call about what he was going to get done before May 23rd. He talked about preparing a goat, a sheep, a pig, several roosters, everything home raised, to throw a big feast. The talk of a lavish celebration made Joey tell him that it wasn't necessary; he would just be happy to be back home, to see everyone alive and healthy. But he knew that nothing could deter his father from doing whatever he said he was going to do, because he had always been like that; that's just who he was.

When he got off the phone with his father, he had one more thing to do. His girlfriend was not privy to his plans. On numerous occasions, she had expressed the desire to meet his family, to visit his home country, but he had often come up with an excuse to put it off to some other time in the future. Sometimes, she would express concern and skepticism that he probably just didn't want her to meet his family because he didn't want her to get her hopes up that they were taking their relationship to the next phase, but in his classic reassuring manner, he would tell her that he just needed time to plan something grandiose and meaningful for her first time meeting his family, her first trip to Cameroon.

So, he called her.

Hey, babe," she answered.

"How's your day going?"

"Pretty good! How about yours? Aren't you supposed to be teaching right now?"

"No, it's my planning period, and they have an awards program at the elementary school; so, I don't have to teach those babies today. I wanted to talk to you before my next class begins, just to hear your beautiful voice and to tell you something that I've been thinking about lately."

"Awe, that's so sweet of you, JJ. So, what have you been thinking about?"

"I just got off the phone with my father, and I told him that you and I will be visiting on May 23rd."

It took her a minute to comprehend what he had said.

"Wait, you mean as in me and you going to Cameroon to see your family? Please tell me that's what you mean, because I've been dying for that to happen for a very long time," she asked, hoping for confirmation that what she had just heard him say was exactly what she had heard.

"That's correct."

She screamed with overwhelming joy, "Oh, my God! Oh, my God!" Then she asked, "When did you make this decision? You didn't hint at this when we spoke for almost three hours last night."

"I have been thinking about it for quite some time. I just wanted to surprise you at the right time."

"It sure is the best surprise ever! I'm so excited; I can't wait to meet your family. I feel like I already know so much about your parents and siblings and even your grandparents from speaking with you over the past four years, but next month I'll finally be able to put faces to the names."

"I can't wait to take you to meet them either. I'll call you tonight, and we'll talk about it in greater detail. I got to go; my students are coming in."

"Have you forgotten? It's Friday, and I'm coming down for the weekend."

"I'm so sorry; I completely forgot. It's been a very hectic week. I'm glad you're coming to see me, because I have missed you so much! Call me when you get on the road so that I can keep you company till you get here. I love you!"

"I love you more, JJ! See you in a few hours. I'll will pick up something for dinner at the new Mexican restaurant when I get to Cleveland."

"Okay, honey! Bye!"

They spent the next few weeks getting everything that would be needed for their voyage to Mbengwi, Cameroon, including a travel visa for Emily, plane tickets, several vaccines for both of them, appropriate clothing for tropical climate, a huge collection of books, magazines, movies, and music for entertainment, and some amazing gifts for his family members. A lot of cash to spend on travel inside Cameroon and for other miscellaneous expenses also needed to be sorted out.

———

Their journey to Africa started with a shorter flight from Memphis to Newark, NJ on a United Airlines plane. From there, they caught a Brussels Airlines flight that took them across the Atlantic Ocean to Brussels, Belgium on the longest phase of their trip, about 10 hours. Much of the literature they had bought came in handy on the flight. The remaining 3255 miles from the chocolate capital of the world to the economic capital of Cameroon, Douala, lasted 6 hours and 50 minutes. He switched his window seat for her middle one when the plane crossed the Mediterranean Sea and began flying over Africa, so that she could catch glimpses of the beautiful mountains, valleys, forests, rivers, modern and traditional architectures, as well as other unique features of the continent that could be admired from several thousand feet above.

Finally, at 8:45 pm, the aircraft touched down at the Douala International Airport. Among frequent travelers to Cameroon, the airport was notorious for deliberate and even criminal inefficiencies by employees, including police and custom officers whose terrible job performance frequently resulted in massive bottlenecks in the City's suffocating heat. For example, the custom officers would stop a passenger for some of the most ridiculous motives. If someone had two cellphones, it was a big problem as they would be suspicious of the person's intentions. If a passenger was carrying many books, they would have to explain to the men in khaki why they loved reading so much. If someone had many pairs of shoes in his or her luggage, he or she would need to explain to them why they needed all the shoes. If a person had two or more laptops or more than one piece of any other electronic gadget, the officers automatically assumed that he or she was up to no good, probably attempting to smuggle the items into the country.

Consequently, the custom officers would make the owner pay a highly arbitrary amount of custom duty on what they considered superfluous items, although the money would never make it to the state's coffers. It would simply be split among the police and custom agents who caught the "illegal" activity.

Thus, because Joey and Emily were traveling with several pieces of both electronics and fashion that were intended as gifts to family and friends, in addition to their own personal items, he knew that they would be ripe targets of the unscrupulous law enforcement officials, unless he lied to them that the items belonged to her.

Cameroonians are generally nice to, and even protective of their guests, especially the White ones. Even when some of the latter visitors treat the citizens of their host country with tremendous disdain and disregard, the cruelty is never reciprocated. Hospitality towards strangers, regardless of their origin and their behavior, is standard in Cameroon.

Therefore, Joey briefly coached Emily on what to do and say when they got to the agents. He was standing behind her in a long line of exhausted passengers who were waiting to retrieve their luggage and get out of the steaming airport. After one and a half hours, it was her turn to have her belongings cleared.

"Welcome to Cameroon," a female inspector of police said to the American, while checking her passport.

"Thank you! How're you doing?" Emily asked.

"Fine, thank you! Is this your luggage?"

"Yes, and the other three suitcases."

The police officer beckoned two customs agents to help her place the pieces of luggage on a long table, and they began to rummage through everything. Without any questions asked, Emily added, "The suitcases contain presents for the friends that I am visiting in Mbengwi and Yaounde."

"Okay, everything looks good! Enjoy your stay in Cameroon. Do you need help carrying these out of the airport? We can get some guys to help you. If you need a taxi, they would help you with that as well," one of the agents offered.

"That would be nice; thank you very much. You guys are the nicest customs agents and police officers I've ever met!" Emily said as the officers were putting the items back together and zipping up the suitcases. One of them ordered someone to bring a cart to transport the visitor's luggage out of the airport.

Then, it was Joey's turn. Like magic, all the warmth and politeness he had seen shown to the White lady, disappeared from the faces of the agents.

"Passport!" the police officer barked without even looking at him. No greetings, no "Welcome to Cameroon!"—nothing nice. She checked his passport and found nothing amiss in it, then she asked for his certificate of vaccination. He was about to point out the fact that she didn't ask that of the American who was ahead of him when something told him to let it go.

He pulled a yellow international certificate of vaccination out of his pocket and handed it to the cop, who took a cursory look at the pages and said that there was no record of BCG, the tuberculosis shot, in it.

"I'm sorry, but I got the BCG vaccine in 2009 before leaving Cameroon, but it was not recorded in that document. I was given a receipt instead. You can see the spot on my arm where I was given the shot," he said as he was rolling up his sleeves to show the officer the scar that was caused by the jab.

"Where's the receipt?"

"I didn't think that it would be needed. No one has ever asked me for it since the day I was vaccinated, so it's among my other personal documents at home in the United States."

Wrong answer. He had gotten himself into a hole that

might be hundreds of dollars deep.

"You need to get a BCG shot before entering Cameroon. It's the law, and I'm just enforcing it as written," she said, still not looking at him.

He tried to explain that the vaccine was good for about 20 years, so it would be dangerous for him to take another TB jab after just 4 years from the date he got the first one, but the lady cop was not interested in anything he was saying.

By that time, the people in line behind him were starting to yell at him to hurry up. Thus, he asked the officer, "Is the vaccine administered here at the airport?" but she did not respond.

Then someone in the line mentioned something he didn't quite catch entirely, but the word "pay" was clear enough.

So, he asked the officer, "How much is the BCG shot?"

With her eyes looking down at something on her phone, she uttered, "100,000 francs CFA." That was about $200. As he was contemplating what to do, the person behind him yelled, "My brother, just give them what they want so that we can get out of this hot airport, for God's sake!"

He took $40 out of his wallet and placed it in front of the lady and said, "That's all I have left."

She let the money sit there for a moment, and then, acting as if she was being forced into a transaction that she wanted no part in, she picked it up and slipped it into her pocket.

That payment took care of everything, even his suitcase was cleared without examination.

Joey was livid about the way the officers had treated him, but their behavior did not surprise him. Custom agents and police officers at ports of entry in Cameroon were unscrupulously corrupt. In fact, to get assigned to one of the gateways to the nation was a significant accomplishment that could get even a first-grade officer more money in one year than they would ever make in their lifetime through legitimate means. Because of the lucrative nature of an airport, seaport, or boarder assignment, custom and police officers were known to pay a lot of money in bribes to land a position at any of the locations. And while there, they would do anything to recuperate their investment and then some. That was the Cameroon Joey had left four years earlier, and sadly, nothing had changed, except for the boldness in the way those with a sworn duty to serve and protect the public were carrying out their corrupt practices. He was ashamed and embarrassed for Emily to witness such brazen malfeasance by law enforcement agents in his home country.

The outside of the Douala international airport that night was not any less chaotic and humid than the inside. Passengers on Joey's flight and other planes that had arrived earlier were flooding out into the narrow, crowded driveway, while other individuals were dragging their luggage hurriedly into the airport to catch a flight, and everyone was doing his or her best to dodge the aggressive taxis, private cars, and motorcycles that seemed to have no regard for the pedestrians rushing in and out of the airport. Joey and Emily managed to get across the driveway and found a spot on the other side to see if they could hail a cab, but everyone that came by was already occupied. The guy who transported their luggage offered to go farther towards the area where the taxis got into the airport so as to catch one before other passengers got it. Minutes later, a cab stopped in front of Joey and Emily, and the luggage guy alighted from it and told them to get in while he loaded their belongings. His clients were so happy with his services that they gave him a significant tip.

By the time they made it out of the airport, it was already 10:30 pm, so, they decided to spend the night in Douala at the Akwa Palace Hotel. The hotel staff were extremely warm and welcoming, especially to Joey's companion. From the moment the taxi pulled up in front of the impressive facility, they rolled out their five-star treatment. Joey couldn't count how many times they asked, "Madame, vous allez bien?" or "Madame, vous voulez quelque chose?" They cared more about the well-being and satisfaction of the foreigner than they did her Cameroonian companion who was conspicuously either her boyfriend or her husband, but he was neither surprised nor upset, because he understood that they were simply acting Cameroonian, ensuring that their expatriate guest was one hundred percent comfortable and happy. It reminded him of the countless times that his cousins would visit his family when school got out for the summer vacation, and, when the time came for them to return to school in their respective cities, his parents would buy all of their guests' school supplies, in addition to clothes, shoes, and other necessary items before asking what their own children needed to start the school year. Joey and his siblings would give their parents the list of what they needed, and, just like they often predicted, after looking at all the items on the lists, their parents would say, "We'll get them at the end of the month," which in most cases was the end of September, three weeks after school started on the first Monday of that month. There was never any money left after all the shopping for the supplies and necessities of the cousins.

After making it to their room on the second floor of the hotel, Joey and Emily quickly took a shower, changed clothes, and returned downstairs to a restaurant as they were famished. The staff there were very nice, but as expected, they were extra nice to the American. They didn't even want her to endure the pain of reading the menu. While Joey was going over every line item on it, she got everything read, translated into English, and described with apt demonstrations to her.

"I can get used to this royal treatment," she said jokingly.

"They would feed you your food, if you let them," he responded, getting jealous.

"I'll get the ndole with sweet plantains and a bottle of the Cabernet de Sauvignon to share with my boyfriend," she said, smiling.

She chose the traditional Cameroonian dish because she

had fallen in love with it the very first time she had it almost two years earlier during a trip to Maryland with Joey and her parents. Mr. and Mrs. Goldman liked it too, so much that they asked the owner of the Roger Milla Restaurant for the recipe and where to get the necessary ingredients, which they acquired that same day. After numerous attempts over the following months, both Mrs. Goldman and her daughter perfected their Ndole cooking skills.

Joey ordered something else that he had not eaten in more than six years, the Mbongo Tchobi, a black, thick, tomato-based, spicy, and velvety sauce that was extremely popular among the Bassa people in Cameroon. However, just like his companion, he got sweet plantains as his side.

While they sat there waiting for their food, she complimented the hospitality and warmth of the locals, something she had heard about, but was excited to be witnessing in real time. From the luggage guy at the airport to the cab driver, and to the hotel staff, everyone they had come in contact with was exceptionally nice to her.

"That's the Cameroonian way," Joey said.

The midnight dinner was, as expected, uniquely delicious. Because of the six-hour time difference, they did not feel sleepy, as they usually would be getting off work in America when it was midnight in Cameroon.

The restaurant, which was accustomed to receiving western travelers and airline crews arriving late at night, remained open until the early hours of the morning. Thus, they ordered another bottle of wine and took their time drinking while admiring the beautiful scenery outside the window. The waiters returned to their table so many times to check on them, mostly on Emily, and when they were finally feeling the effects of jet lag combined with the impact of the alcohol, they stood up to leave. Emily insisted that they give the waiters a $200 tip for their exceptional service.

As they were walking to their room, Joey explained to her

that, unlike in the United States where tipping was expected because the waiters depended heavily on it for income, in Cameroon tipping was purely voluntary as the bill for a meal also included the cost of the service, and the waiters were paid a fixed salary monthly, whether the restaurant did well or not. Nevertheless, the salary was not the greatest, ranging from 74,000 CFA Francs to 218,000 CFA Francs a month depending on the type of restaurant, low-end or high-class. Thus, the $200 tip they had left for their two waiters at the superior quality restaurant was about 108,000 CFA Francs, which was ¼ of the monthly salary of each of them.

They woke up at 10:00 am and got ready for the fourth and final phase of the journey to Joey's hometown. For that, they rented a mid-size sedan, a Toyota Camry, that was clean and in excellent condition for $600. It came with a driver whose name was George. The latter loaded the car with his passengers' luggage. Because there wasn't enough room in the trunk to hold everything they had, some of the luggage was placed behind the driver's seat.

With everything thus loaded up, the passengers invited George to eat breakfast with them at the restaurant from the night before. They had slices of baguette with omelet and slices of pineapple and mango with coffee. While they were eating, they asked their chauffeur questions about the route he would take, the duration of the journey, any stops on the way, etc.

They finished eating an hour later, paid their bill and left another generous tip, and George asked with enthusiasm, "Are you guys ready?"

"Yes, we're ready!" Emily responded excitedly.

George drove for hours through the beautiful Littoral Region towards the amazing and breathtaking hills of the Menoua Division in the Western Region, and after almost five hours, they made it to the mesmerizing city of Bamenda in the Northwest Region. They were just 30 minutes away from

Mbengwi. The driver eased the car into a Shell gas station on the famous Commercial Avenue in the capital city of the region to refuel it. Joey also needed to rush into a supermarket on the avenue to get a few items like cases of wine, whiskey, loaves of the delicious Kumba bread, and other things that he knew his parents would appreciate from the city. He was going to give some of the wine and whiskey to friends and former teachers who were the most impactful during his days in elementary, middle, and high school. As a sign of respect and appreciation, Cameroonians often give gifts of fine drinks to individuals who played a remarkable role in their success.

Before leaving Bamenda, Joey also went into a phonebooth to call his father to let him know that they were half an hour away. His dad was feverishly excited at the news.

George got his passengers to GRA Mbengwi at exactly 4:55 pm on May 25th, 2012. Tired of waiting for their guests and eager to see them, Joey's entire family, neighbors and several friends had left the house to go stand on the side of the road, about 900 feet away.

"They were supposed to have arrived by now. I wonder what delayed them," Joey's father wondered out loud.

"Everyone be patient; they will be here at any moment," his mom responded reassuringly.

Because they were waiting for one of the familiar cars that transported passengers from Mbengwi to Bamenda daily, no one paid attention to the blue Camry when it slowed down and came to a stop right in front of them. The front passenger door opened, and everyone recognized the subject of long hours of waiting, and screaming with tremendous joy, they all dashed towards him at the same time, almost knocking him over. They hugged and kissed him for a couple of minutes, and in the midst of all the excitement, everyone, including Joey, forgot that there were other people in the car, one of them being a long-awaited guest as well.

Joey opened the rear right passenger door for Emily to

alight from the car. As soon as she came out of the sedan, just like he had anticipated, everyone's attention immediately turned to her, and they treated her with such familiarity like they had known her for decades. They hugged, held, and kissed her jubilantly.

There was no need to get back in the car for the short distance to the house; thus, everyone, a crowd of over 25 people walked behind it as George slowly drove the 900 feet and parked the Camry in front of the modest residence of the Jumessis.

The 3000 square-foot cinder block home with aluminum roofing sat at the center of a one-acre piece of land. It had five big bedrooms, one large living room and two bathrooms in it, but the kitchen was a two-room structure of similar materials outside, behind the main house. Like almost everyone in the region, Joey's parents used the firewood kitchen for cooking and to hang the products from their farms to dry, including corn, beans, and peanuts. Unlike the main house that had beautiful plywood ceilings in all the rooms and all around the exterior, the kitchen didn't have a ceiling. Several wood poles hung horizontally from the roof, and they served the purpose of holding the produce that would be hung on them to dry. The exterior of both buildings was sky blue, while a light-yellow color was used to paint the inside, although the smoke from the firewood fireplace that was used to cook had turned the walls of the kitchen black in certain places.

Joey's family did exactly what his father mentioned to him in the phone call four weeks earlier. A significant ceremony was planned to welcome him and his girlfriend home. Scores of white plastic chairs were set up under a huge white and blue tent in the yard while multiple plastic tables of same color as the chairs were joined together to form one long table on which multiple Cameroonian delicacies were displayed, including ekwang, achu, fufu and eru, ndole, porridge cocoyam, known in the region as nang tarre, sweet plantains, fufu and njama njama, koki, and rice and goat stew.

Additionally, crates of beer and boxes of wine and liquor could be seen stacked on the veranda as the honorees were led up the steps and into the living room that had been prepared for the celebration. There were chairs lined up against the four walls and down the corridor that led to the posterior veranda and to the to the backyard kitchen. Just like out front, several tables were linked together to spread out similar foods and drinks as outside. Meanwhile, tunes by one of Joey's favorite singers, the popular Congolese musician, JB Mpiana, could be heard blasting from the wall-mounted loudspeakers.

When the guests' luggage had been secured in one of the bedrooms, Joey's father instructed everyone to have a seat. He was ready to get the party started with a speech.

"I want to thank the almighty God for bringing our son, Joey, and his girlfriend, Emily, home to Mbengwi safely after he's been away in America for almost four years. The lord knows how much we've missed him! There were times when I wondered if I'd ever set my eyes on him again because, as you all know, I've been sick for some time now. But, by the grace of God, he's finally here with his woman that we've heard so many wonderful things about," the father said, then he turned to Emily and continued. "Emily, Joey has told us how you have supported him and have looked out for him since you have been together, and, on behalf of our entire family, I want to thank you from the bottom of my heart. You're a good woman, and we pray that God would keep you and our son together forever!"

He did not want to transition to item 11 without allowing Joey's mother who was standing right next to him to say something, so he asked as her, "You want to say something Mami Joey?"

"Yes, I just want to thank God for bringing my boy home to me again. I've been praying for this day for the past three plus years, hoping that the lord would allow us to see him again, and he has answered our prayers in a very big way. Not only did he bring Joey back to us, but he also brought Emily who has been taking such great care of him in America. Isn't God good? He is a wonderful God; thank you lord!" she shouted to a unanimous "Amen" from the audience.

Joey and Emily too spoke briefly, mostly thanking everyone for the warm welcome and expressing how eagerly they were looking forward to spending the next few weeks resting in Cameroon after several grueling months of work and school.

After all the speeches, the catholic priest who had been invited to the event said a thanksgiving prayer and blessed the food. The celebration lasted all night with more people joining the large crowd that was already there when the honorees arrived. There was more than enough to eat and drink and plenty of great *Makossa, Ndombolo, Ben skin, Assiko, and Bikutsi* to dance off the calories.

Everyone wanted to dance with Emily, and she did not mind. She was having so much fun dancing to the respective genres even though she was mostly off-beat, to the amusement of crowd. Joey's sisters and parents also seem to be having tremendous enjoyment teaching her how to dance Makossa and Ben Skin. At one point, Joey noticed that she had taken off her shoes, rolled up her sleeves and the legs of her pants and she had his mother's *wrapper* around her waist, and she was cutting lose. Several people surrounded her, and they started cheering and applauding and screaming. They were fascinated by the cute White girl who was putting on an impressive spectacle.

Before long, word had spread to the folks in the living room about the show that was going on outside and, within seconds, the room emptied. No one wanted to miss seeing the American lady dancing Ben Skin up close. It was probably a once-in-a-lifetime opportunity for most of them. Cellphone cameras were flashing repeatedly as the captivated spectators wanted to memorialize the experience in pictures.

One can tell when a dancer is really killing it in Africa when the spectators do not just scream and applaud with excitement, but they also start emptying their pockets, purses, and wallets to rain cash on the dancer. That's exactly what people started doing as they were carried away by Emily's spellbinding moves, and when Joey saw them placing bills and coins on her forehead, he stepped into the middle of the circle and whispered in her ear that it was a sign of appreciation, admiration, and encouragement. He did not want her to make any connections in her mind to the practice in the United States where guys make dollar bills rain on ladies in gentlemen's clubs.

By 2:00 am, both honorees and the parents were very tired, and they excused themselves for the night, even though many people were still acting like the party was just beginning.

The guestroom was reserved for Emily, while Joey shared his old bedroom with his younger brother, Steve, who had taken it over when he had left for the United States. The two of them talked for some time as Steve had many questions about life in the country of Uncle Sam and wanted to know if his older brother had brought the laptop that he had asked for.

"Let me catch some sleep, Steve; you're acting like I'm going back tonight. I'll be here for four weeks. You'll have plenty of time with me to get answers to any questions you want to ask me. You also have to wait till the morning to find out what Emily and I got for you," he told his brother after realizing that the latter wanted to talk all night.

As it was customary in the Jumessi household, the mother woke up early to fix breakfast. That morning, she was assisted by her daughters, Cecilia and Marie. They made his favorite Cameroonian breakfast consisting for *puff-puff*, beans, and pap. They also made omelets to eat with bread and assorted fruits, just in case Emily did not like her boyfriend's preferred breakfast. There was coffee, tea, and hot cocoa available to drink.

When they were done preparing, the lady of the house personally went to wake up the rest of the household and summoned them to brush their teeth, wash their faces, and report to the table for breakfast. She got Emily to try every single item on the menu, like every Cameroonian mother does with her guests. In fact, not only do they make the guest try everything, but they also keep adding food to the guest's plate and expect him or her to empty it clean. Luckily for the host, the American found all the menu items extremely delicious and even asked for more of the puff-and beans with a side of the pap.

When everyone was done eating, Emily helped Joey's sisters clear the table while the rest of the family chatted. When the girls returned, Joey quickly changed the topic and asked, "Are you all ready to see what Emily and I brought for you?"

There was a unanimous "Yes" around the table.

Emily and Joey went and got the suitcases filled with gifts and returned to the living room. Each of his siblings received a Dell laptop, while his father got an iPad, blood pressure and glucose monitors, pairs of jeans and Nike tennis shoes. For his mother, they got a couple of Michael Kors purses, designer dresses, shoes, and jewelry. It was like Christmas had come early to the Jumessi household and everyone was overwhelmed with joy and full of gratitude for the generous givers, especially Emily.

While the recipients were busy trying and checking out their new acquisitions, Joey announced that he would like to give Emily a tour of his hometown. They took a shower and got dressed for the ride around his hometown. His older sister, Cecilia, who had arrived from Yaounde too the previous day to welcome them, asked if she could join them on the tour, and they were glad to have her ride along.

Their first stop down the street was at the Government

Bilingual School, G.B.S., Mbengwi where all the Jumessi kids attended grades 1-7. The campus had not changed a lot in decades; most of the architecture and landscape was the same as it was when Joey had graduated 15 years prior, although a couple of new classrooms could be seen near the *dining shed.* In all, there were seven buildings on the campus, all of which were constructed with cinderblocks and were showing signs of the 50 plus years that they had been standing. A few of them were plastered and painted white, while the rest were not. Additionally, the classrooms that were painted happened to be the ones that had doors and window shutters, while all the remaining classrooms didn't have any.

Each of the classrooms had 25 to 30 two-seater wooden desks, some of which had been there for three decades. On one of the desks in his 7th grade classroom, Joey could barely make out the words "class of 1980." Also, as old as each building, was the cement, wall-to-wall blackboard that was in front of the room. Joey recalled his teacher writing on it and inviting students from time to time to come and show his or her peers how to solve a problem. He frequently had the honor of being called to the board to walk the class through a task while the instructor looked on and provided feedback. Those memories brought happy tears to his eyes.

He was equally emotional as he thought about all the years that he attended G.B.S Mbengwi, about his teachers, and all the friends he made during those years, some of whom had passed away. He knew a few former classmates who had gone on to great academic accomplishments, but he wondered what everyone else had become.

When they made it to class five, he told the story of his first ever crush, how he would pass notes to her in the classroom via a friend who he discovered after four months that he was not giving the notes to the girl because he wanted her for himself.

One day, Joey gathered enough courage to speak to her as

she was walking home from school. He asked her why she had not been responding to any of his notes, at least 60 of them, and she told him that he was lying, because she had not received any.

"So, what did you do when you found out that your friend had been deceiving you?" Emily managed to ask as both she and Cecilia were dying laughing.

"We fell out. We were no longer friends, especially after she confronted him for playing both of us, because, as it turned out, she too had been telling him how I was cute and smart, and how she would like me to help her with arithmetic and nature study assignments sometimes, but he had been keeping all of that from me."

"You all were too young to be caught up in a love triangle," Emily joked.

"Well, I would say that, because I started that early, I have had a lot of experience that has made me a better man for you today," he teased as they continued to the orchard behind the francophone classrooms.

While they were looking at the guava trees, Emily noticed the steep valley that was behind the school, and she wanted to look at it. Thus, all three of them found a safe spot on the edge of the mountain and admired the beautiful vegetation and rock formations that were down below. He told her stories of the days when he and his friends used to take benches out of classroom, flip them over, and three to five of them would sit on the flipped bench and glide thousands of feet down the valley to harvest mango, pick palm nuts, and drink *palm wine* when they suspected the owners of these treats might not be on their farms. They were lucky most of the times, but one day, their luck ran out, and they were caught and brought to the headmasters' office while they were still under the influence of the gallons of palm wine that they had drunk.

"Oh, my God! You all were some terrible kids! How old were you when that happened?" Emily asked.

"I was 12."

"Did your parents find out about what you had done?"

"Of course, and my mother almost killed me on that day. She beat me to a pulp using anything she could find. She used a belt, and when that didn't deliver the sting she wanted, she grabbed a pestle out of the mortar, and when that broke when she mistakenly hit the wall, she just took off both of her shoes and started swinging with both hands until I fell on the floor and pretended to be unconscious. Needless to say that I learned a major lesson from that experience."

"I bet you did," his sister said, and both girls were laughing at the thought of Joey feigning to be dead just to stop a whipping.

They left G.B.S. and drove to the Government Bilingual High School, G. B.H.S., on the other side of the town where he attended grades 8 to 14.

"It looks like the campus of a major university in the United States," Emily remarked.

They toured the older part of the school which housed the junior high classrooms before heading uphill to the ultra-modern high school complex. Nothing on the G.B.H.S. campus looked like what was shown on videos soliciting donations in America for schools in Africa. The gymnasium, library, science laboratories, cafeteria, clinic, sports arenas, dormitories, classrooms, offices, residences for the administrators, and overall landscaping were magnificent. Emily was so impressed by the campus that she started taking pictures and videos of features of the school and posting them on social media and sending some directly to her family and friends back home.

On their way back home, they stopped in Mile 17 to see the Abbi Falls, a major touristic attraction that brought thousands of admirers annually to Mbengwi from as far as Europe, North and South America, Asia, and Australia. The massive rocks scattered around the valley and the uniquely beautiful vegetation that could be seen down the valley were breathtaking. The three tourists sat atop a huge rock that was about the size of an average living room in the United States for Emily to take pictures while contemplating God's wondrous creations in front of her.

Two side-by-side flows of water, about 10 feet apart from each other, one major and the other minor, made up the waterfall. The former, River Abbi, meandered its way across the Northwest Region and fed the hydroelectric dam that was less than a mile away from where the admirers were sitting. About 65% completed by 1970, the dam, in which Joey learned to swim when he was just 3 years old, was forever abandoned by the government, like thousands of other state projects around Cameroon, although official documents showed them fully paid for, completed, inspected, delivered, and totally functional. What that meant was many corrupt and unscrupulous contractors, politicians, and government officials syphoned public funds with impunity, while the poor citizens for whom the services were intended were condemned to go for decades, and even a lifetime without basic needs.

During the rainy season, from March to September, the volume of the River Abbi would swell exponentially, thus causing the water to overflow its banks, and during that period, the flow of the river into the waterfall would be incredibly massive and powerful such that it would cause widespread foam that looked like a white carpet covering the water surface down below the valley.

Meanwhile, the second current flowing into Abbi Falls was a less voluminous body of water called Tugabbi. It originated from an underground source that was about two miles away, right below the district office and the police station and slowly snaked its way towards the catholic school and beyond, until it emptied into the valley to merge with River Abbi.

There was a spot behind the catholic primary school that was as large as an Olympic swimming pool, and kids attending the Christian school and others from G.B.S, about three miles away, used to get together there to swim during and after school hours. Additionally, students who had a beef with one another used to meet there to settle scores. The aquatic amusement scene was also a favorite rendezvous spot for teenage lovers. Joey couldn't count the times when he went there between 5th and 7th grades for all the above-mentioned reasons, especially the last one.

After savoring the view of Abbi Falls, the trio left for the local market called Mbon in Mile 18. Joey had told Emily about the juicy and succulent mangoes that he used find there when he lived in Mbengwi, and she had added them to the list of things that she wanted to taste before leaving Cameroon. Although there were stores in the square-shaped, mall-like market, most of the trading happened in the open-air courtyard and outside the gates of the facility. People could find just about anything at Mbon, including clothing, food, electronics, kitchen utensils and appliances, building materials, alcoholic and soft drinks, prescription drugs, groceries, live animals, etc.

As soon as they got out of the car outside the main entrance to the market, Joey noticed the hustle and bustle that he knew about the central shopping square was conspicuously absent. It was still afternoon, but many of the stores were closed, while the few that were open, had very scanty shelves. A significant number of the benches on which food traders exposed their produce in the huge courtyard were concerningly bare. When asked what had happened to the once jewel of Mbengwi, the lady who sold Joey the mangoes, a graduate of the University of Buea with a master's degree in accounting, attributed the dizzying decline of the shopping center to the worsening social and economic crises that was impacting the entire nation. She said that the hardship was hitting the Anglophone areas the hardest due to decades of the national government's marginalization of these regions to the advantage of the Francophone parts of the country.

"In fact, hundreds of graduate school dissertations and numerous publications have documented and criticized the fact that upwards of 90% of political and government officials in Cameroon are Francophones, including a substantial number of the administrative, judicial, business, healthcare, and law enforcement leaders in the Anglophone regions.

"The exclusion of Anglophones from the mainstream of the political, economic, judicial, and social power nationally and even in the English-speaking zones is the cause of severe tension that is putting a severe strain on social and economic productivity," the lady lamented.

"That's been going on since the eighties, and one would expect things to have improved by now," supported Joey.

"No, they have instead become worse. For instance, imagine being the defendant in a case in a courtroom in your own hometown before a judge and a prosecutor who could barely speak or understand English, the language of this Anglophone region. What do you think the outcome of the case would be for the defendant? That's happening to thousands of individuals, some of whom could be innocent," she slammed.

"How's that allowed to happen?" Emily asked, scandalized.

"Well, like he said, it's been going on for decades, and you've not even heard all of it. Imagine going into a local government building in Mbengwi or Banso to get a copy of your birth certificate or to obtain a construction permit or a land title or to apply for a passport or a driver license and the government official in charge doesn't even understand you because he or she does not speak English. What would you do? Furthermore, imagine going to the police station in Bamenda to file a report about a crime that has occurred to you or any of your loved ones, but neither the commissioner nor his subordinates speak English fluently. Same thing at a bank in the Northwest and Southwest Regions. Imagine going into a financial institution to do a transaction but everybody working there speaks only French. Finally, imagine being sick and needing immediate medical attention, but the doctors and the nurses at the hospital you go to in these areas cannot understand English in that moment of life and death. I'm telling you, my brother, because of the systemic marginalization of Anglophones in this country, things have gotten frightful. That, in addition to the systemic nepotism, nativism, tribalism, and corruption, has made getting a job for people like us in any sector, whether public or private, virtually impossible. Nothing is based on merit or any objective criteria. You have parents in high positions looking out for their children, while their kids in turn look out for their buddies and other acquaintances, and all these people trade their access to the circle of power to the highest bidders. Look at me; I've a master's degree in accounting and I was in my second year in the doctoral program, but I had to quit school because I didn't have the money to continue, and I couldn't find a job anywhere. I am now selling fruits here in this empty market to make ends meet for me and my aging, sick parents, but this is not working. That's how the Francophones have maintained their overwhelming dominance over every single aspect of life in this nation, and it has resulted in the dire state of affairs that you see across the Anglophone cities, towns and villages," she elaborated before making an ominous prediction about what could happen to the country with the backs of most Anglophones against the wall, with almost everyone in the two English-speaking regions at a breaking point.

As they left the market, Joey thought about what the unemployed, highly educated lady, Irene, had predicted, and it brought chills to his body. Every Francophone living in the Anglophone cities, towns, and villages, along with their property and everything remotely linked to the oppressive government would be prime targets in the insurrection that she was almost certain was going to happen at any time, if things didn't change for the better. That meant, even his own family would be in the eye of the storm, and while they were narrowly spared the worst during a minor uprising of Anglophones in the early nineties, he didn't think that they could be passed over if the type of conflict Irene talked about broke out, because the predicament of Anglophones had only compounded.

In her words, "Imagine someone you know is the cause of you not being able to find a job, afford food, clothing, a roof over your head, means to send your children to school, basic healthcare, and other fundamental human necessities. Imagine this person also exploiting all the natural resources from your own backyard, but he doesn't deem you worthy enough to invest some of the proceeds to develop your area. Imagine this person enacting laws and policies about every aspect of life in their language and having them applied to his advantage. Now imagine you see this person and their loved ones and their prized possessions, mostly exposed and vulnerable. What would you do if you had nothing to lose? Would you be able to resist the temptation to follow the path of your rage?"

From every indication, there was a lot of anger built up for an extremely long time in Anglophone Cameroon, and that could explode with incredibly devastating consequences at any moment, and Joey's family in Mbengwi could bear the brunt. The town was the only home he and his siblings knew; they were born and bred there. His parents had lived there for more than 40 years, longer than many of those in it in 2012, but he wasn't sure that fact could even be considered if the Anglophones rose up to rid themselves of the predominantly Francophone government and everything associated with French-speaking Cameroon. He was deeply worried about the future of his family and his hometown, but he tried to stay calm in order not to alarm the guest that he had brought to the country.

The gloominess and abandonment that characterized Mbon Market and its surroundings were also obvious on both sides of the road as George was driving his passengers home via a different route than the one he took the day before. While going towards Njembeng and turning right to climb the steep hill that led to the technical teachers training school, ENIET, Joey noticed that once vibrant and thriving businesses and homes were dilapidated and in ruins. Some of the houses were hard to see because of the bush that had overtaken them. He wondered what had happened to the families that used to live in them. Had they just moved elsewhere in search of a better life, or had the suffering precipitated their untimely death? The impact of the devastating social and economic crises extended farther as the car headed towards the police station and veered off the main road to take the street in front the divisional education office that would lead them back to GRA. An outing that was full of excitement, nostalgia, and anticipation was thus ending in worry and uncertainty.

By the time they got home at 2 pm, the table had been set for a late lunch as everyone was waiting for them to return before they could eat. The spread at the ten-seater mahogany table consisted of *koki* beans with sweet plantains, okra soup with *gari,* and sliced bread with vegetable salad. A few family friends who couldn't make it to the reception the previous day, had shown up while the honorees were still out touring the town. Therefore, lunch wasn't just a bit crowded, but it was also very loud, and that was a welcome distraction for Joey's troubled mind.

After resting and relaxing with his family in Mbengwi for over a week, Joey and Emily left on a two-week trip to several regions in Cameroon. Their first stop was at the birthplace of his parents, in Dschang, a tremendously prosperous college city in the Western Region. They spent a day with his paternal grandparents, Joseph and Rose Kenfack who were 94 and 88-years old respectively according to their birth certificates, although neither of them knew exactly when they were born, because of the non-existence of an effective system for recording and tracking births in the country for most of the 20th century.

The birth certificates of people born during that period state the date of birth as "Around 19..." Thus, both Joseph and Rose were born around 1910 and 1920, and like most people from that era, they were only able to get a high school education. However, they took a lot of pride in making excruciating sacrifices to ensure that their children went much farther in school than they did.

Joey's grandma and grandad were elated to welcome their grandson and his lady. In fact, Joseph took a particular liking for Emily, because she reminded him of Jacqueline Kennedy, the wife of his favorite American president until Barack Obama came. He thought that her face, body and height were similar to the first lady's, in addition to the fact that she was extremely pretty, gorgeous, elegant, and smart.

Joseph invited a dozen of his neighbors to meet his guests from America, and they were very honored. Grandma Rose prepared rice and tomato sauce with fish, and everyone ate to their fill. The bottles of liquor and wine that Joey had bought for his grandfather came in handy at the spontaneous celebration. George was dispatched to fetch a couple of crates of beer to supplement the drinks that were available.

At 8 pm, Joseph told his neighbors that they could each grab another beer or get a refill of the wine or liquor and return to their respective houses, because he wanted to spend some quality time with his grandson and his girlfriend. When all the people left, Joey's grandparents started flooding him and Emily with all kinds of questions, some of which were intentionally personal, intrusive, and uncomfortable. For example, they wanted to know how Emily and Joey met, who made the first move, what people thought about a biracial couple like them, if it was true that biracial couples and their children were frequently the victims of violent attacks in America, if they were going to get married, etc. They continued chatting until late that night.

The next morning, Grandma Rose fixed beans, puff-puff,

and pap for breakfast. The guests devoured the food with relish. In Joey's mind, he was thinking that he should consume as much of his favorite dishes as possible because he might not have the opportunity to taste them again for many years after returning to the United States. When they finished eating, they sat on the veranda facing the street to chat. Because the veranda was about 20 feet from the artery, they could see all the people and vehicles going back and forth on the busy road. They were close enough to hear what passersby were saying to one another. Thus, as they sat there chatting that morning, they picked up what people were saying about Mr. Joseph's grandson and his pretty White girlfriend. Most of the things people said were nice, but a couple of ladies in their thirties could be overheard saying, "What a waste for a fine man like him to go all the way to America to pick a woman, a White one for that matter, when there are many single and worthy ladies here in his own village that would be great for him." Grandma Rose and Grandpa Joseph laughed at what the ladies said, prompting Emily to ask Joey to translate what was said.

"It's not important, honey. Those two ladies said something about guys from here being with ladies from other countries when there are many single women ready to mingle back home."

"They're just jealous. My grandson is free to be with whomever he wants, regardless of her race or ethnicity. We do not discriminate in this family," Grandma Rose said, so loudly that the ladies may have heard her.

Emily was not offended, especially because Joey had done a commendable job of reassuring her that she was the only woman in the whole world that he wanted to be with.

Just before noon, Joey and Emily prepared to depart for his maternal grandmother's house. As they were loading up the car, Grandma Rose whispered in his ear, "She's a very good girl. She would make a fantastic wife for you. Marry her!" He smiled in agreement and hugged her again, the fifth time that morning.

As the car eased out of their front yard, Grandpa Joseph yelled to Emily, "Come back to see us again soon, and don't forget to greet Barack Obama for me!"

"We sure will!" she responded, waving goodbye.

"Your grandparents are really sweet, JJ. Grandpa Joseph is hilarious, and he knows so much about the United States. His admiration of Obama is like that of a five-year-old and their favorite superhero."

"He learned all about the United States from reading everything he could lay his hands on, from listening to the radio, and from watching TV," Joey responded.

They spent the rest of the day with his maternal grandmother who lived five miles away, on the other side of Foto, Dschang. Grandma Josephine was a widow, having lost her husband Richard almost a decade earlier as a result of the actions of some very callous, negligent, and irresponsible medical personnel at the local hospital. He was having a heart attack and needed immediate medical attention, but the doctor and the nurses at the hospital wanted to be paid before they could attend to him. By the time that his son, Joey's uncle, made it to the medical facility to pay the amount of money that they were asking for, Grandpa Richard had given up the ghost.

In America and Europe, that would be a significant scandal that would cost people their medical licenses and the hospital significant sums of money in legal fees and settlement, but in Cameroon, heinous acts like that occurred in hospitals with impunity on a daily basis. His mother and her siblings emptied the savings to sue the hospital and the staff involved, but that lawsuit did not go anywhere. That medical facility, just like more than 90% of the others in the country, was owned by the government, and instances where anyone had ever won a case against the government were as rare as an African country making it to the quarter finals of the FIFA World Cup. Such slim chances did not inspire any medical professional to think twice before doing anything that might endanger the wellbeing of their patients. Anything that put more money into their pockets was fair game.

Grandma Josephine looked slightly younger than her in-laws, and just like the latter, she did not know her exact date of birth. She was short, energetic, dark-skinned, and wrinkled. Her *head tie* did not fully cover her head, so some of her gray hair could be seen, especially the edges. Her matching *kaba* was long, almost touching the floor, but each step she took revealed her white moccasin slippers.

She excitedly rushed to the car as it came to a stop in front of her small house. She opened the door for Joey, and as soon as he alighted, he landed into her wide-opened arms. Then she gently squeezed his jaws, shoulders, and arms with both of her hands as she repeatedly said, "Welcome my child, welcome my husband! I didn't think I would ever see you again." Joey's middle name, Kemdong, was her husband's last name, and since his birth, she always called her grandson "My husband." After lengthily greeting her grandson, she turned towards Emily who had gotten out of the car and was standing nearby.

"You must be Emily; I've heard a lot of wonderful things about you. Welcome to my home," she said as she gave her a big hug. Then she thanked the driver for bringing her guests safely to see her before leading everyone to the veranda of her house to sit down. She called one of Joey's second cousins who lived with her to bring out the boiled fresh peanuts and roasted corn that had been prepared for the guests.

The trio sat on the veranda for hours, until 9:00 pm, chatting. The questions that Grandma Josephine asked her grandson and his gorgeous girlfriend made them think that all the grannies had gotten together to align what they wanted to know about Joey's life in America and his relationship with the really nice White girl. He laughed at some of the questions before responding. For example, she wondered if it was true that White people did not take a shower frequently, which was why they created fragrances to mask their body odor. When he translated that question for Emily, she found it extremely funny.

—

The next morning at breakfast, Grandma Josephine expressed profound gratitude for the new clothes and shoes that Joey and Emily had brought for her. They also gave her money for a new TV set since the one she had was damaged by lightning weeks earlier. As they got ready to leave, she insisted that they take the bags of potatoes and pinto beans that she had packed for them to take to America. Joey told her that both items were in abundant supply in Indianola, but she did not want to hear any excuse for not taking her gifts. "There may be potatoes and beans in America, but they are not your grandmother's!" she emphasized. Thus, Joey told George to load up everything in the car. Just like his paternal grandparents, Grandma Josephine told her grandson that Emily was an impressive lady who would make a wonderful wife for him.

From Dschang, they headed to Buea, the capital of the English-speaking Southwest Region. The day after their arrival, they toured the campus of the University of Buea and from there they went hiking on Mount Fako, one of the tallest mountains in Africa and one of the most active volcanoes in the world. They could not go too far up the geographical feature because of the risk, but everything they were able to see was so beautiful, from the solidified lava formations to the vegetation.

In the evening, they drove down to the picturesque seaside city of Limbe for dinner at a place called Down Beach. The savory smell of seasoned, spicy fresh fish grilled right on the shores of the same waters from which they were caught minutes earlier was mouth-watering. The fish was so delicious that Emily insisted on returning there the next day for lunch and to hang out on the beach. She was so impressed by the natural beauty of Limbe and the warmth of the people that, when the time came to depart for Yaounde, the capital of the nation, she was not ready to leave.

"We will plan to spend more time here when we come next time; I promise," Joey attempted to console her.

"I'll hold you to that, JJ. It's so refreshing here!" she said.

Because Yaounde was 5.5 hours away, they left Limbe at 3 pm in order to arrive before it was too late. Joey told George to fill-up at a gas station in the city while he got some snacks and drinks for the road, to ensure that they did not have to stop anywhere until they reached the political capital of Cameroon.

It was smooth driving out of the Southwest, but when they made it to Dibombari, at the entrance to Douala, the economic capital, Joey was awakened by a loud male voice ordering him in French to roll the window down. It was a gendarmerie officer, the equivalent of the military police in the United States, except for the fact that in Cameroon they did most of the tasks that regular police officers did, including traffic checks, arrests, crowd control, criminal investigations, etc. They, along with police officers, were commonly called *les mange milles* because, as termites were to the wood frame of a house, so were the gendarmerie and police officers in Cameroon to the contents of the pockets, purses, and wallets of civilians. They would pull over a vehicle for no cause, and if they couldn't find a motive to extract a bribe from the driver and the passengers, they would create one.

Thus, while one officer was asking George for his license, registration, insurance, etc., another one was ordering Emily and Joey to hand him their identification. Her American passport and her visa to enter Cameroon were quickly checked and she was cleared. Then the officer paged through Joey's passport a couple of times, shook his head and then asked to see his national identity card.

"I'm sorry officer, I don't have my national identity card on me because I thought that my valid passport was sufficient identification, according to the law," Joey countered in English, which made an already bad situation worse.

The officer put the passport into his breast pocket and walked away without saying a word.

Meanwhile his colleague, who had checked all the car documents and found them to be in order, threw them on the hood of the Camry in disappointment.

Clearly understanding what was going on and in a bid to avoid wasting more time, Joey asked George for a thousand francs and walked over to the officer who was already raising his right hand and blowing his whistle to stop another prey. The agent of the law openly, shamelessly collected the money and returned the travel document. Case closed.

Fuming with rage as he returned to the car, Joey asked George if he could tell what station the officers were from, just in case he wanted to file a grievance for bribery and corruption.

"That's a great idea, babe. Brazen crooked behavior like this has to be reported to their superior," Emily said, provoking laughter so profuse that the driver almost lost control of the car.

"What's so funny?" she asked in astonishment.

"Do you think that their boss doesn't know what his officers are doing? What do you think happens to all the money that is collected at these checkpoints? Let me tell you that at the end of their shift, they go back to the office and split the cash with the boss, with him getting the lion's share. And if they did not bring back enough dough, their commander would be upset, and he would assume that they were not aggressive, greedy, and ruthless enough. Consequently, he would assign them desk duty and send out other unscrupulous agents who would not be too nice to the drivers and passengers the next day," George explained, and added, "So, if you go to file a report with the commander, he would pretend to listen to you and may even act shocked and angry, but, as soon as you leave, your report would be pigeonholed and you would have wasted your precious time."

Wasting precious time was not something that Joey was going to do, not when they had more than four hours of traveling ahead of them and it would soon start getting dark. With palpable frustration, he said, "Let's just go on to Yaounde, but something has to be done to stop this shameless corruption. It's a cancer that's metastasizing rapidly, and it will bring this country to its knees one day. Maybe I could write an article or book about my experience and encourage other victims and sympathizers to be vocal about this evil. We could start a movement to expose and shame individuals, institutions, and organizations that engage in underhanded, unscrupulous practices." Both Emily and George agreed with him.

As a result of the delay that was caused by the disreputable gendarmerie officers at the entrance to Douala, they made it to the city of the seven hills at 10:50 pm. As always, the capital city looked beautiful with its numerous impressive buildings and countless structures under construction or undergoing renovation. Just like in Douala and other cities in Francophone Cameroon, such as Bafoussam, Kribi, Garoua, Maroua, Ebolowa, Ngaoundere, and Bertoua, the continuous construction of modern infrastructure by the government, private organizations, and individuals in Yaounde reflected the economic prosperity and the priorities of those involved. The city that Joey left in 2009 had changed significantly. More streets had been paved. More double-digit story buildings were sprouting from the ground all over Yaounde. Bigger supermarkets and strings of shops with attractive, colorful lighting lined every street that they passed. Bustling places where he used to hang out such as at Mini Ferme, Cinema le Capitol, Avenue Kennedy, Bonamoussadi, Carefour Biyemassi, etc. had transformed tremendously into bigger, better, more modern entertainment and recreational venues. The capital city was breathing. Its massive lungs were sucking in huge gulps of air. Legitimately acquired money and the proceeds from corruption and other unrighteous practices were fueling the breathtaking blossoming that was occurring in Yaounde and in the other French-speaking cities.

"It's definitely like night and day, the difference between the Cameroon where we've spent the past couple of weeks and the one we have just arrived in," Emily remarked.

"Yes, if a foreigner visiting Cameroon for the first time were to tour only Yaounde or Douala or any of the other big francophone cities, they would have the impression that Cameroon is a very prosperous, stable, and thriving country, but that would be incredibly erroneous. You're getting to see both sides of the coin," George pointed out to Emily.

After burning an hour just riding through the streets of Yaounde and taking in the remarkable changes that were taking place, Joey told George to head to the Hilton Hotel, their home for the next five days.

The Hilton in Yaounde, the only one in the nation, was one of the most beautiful hotels in Africa. It had 248 guest rooms, 18 meeting rooms, four fantastic restaurants, shops, a couple of nightclubs, and numerous other facilities for exercising, business, recreation, and relaxation. Heads of State, company executives, show business superstars, and everyone with money stayed at the Hilton located on the 20th May Boulevard, a stone's throw from the prime minister's office. These personalities were not just drawn there by the fantastic rooms and impressive amenities, but also by the fact that its location at the center of the city offered access to everything people like them sought, including powerful government officials, politicians, business leaders, amazing restaurants, fabulous entertainment venues, and bustling commercial centers. The ideal location of the Hilton was what prompted Joey to choose it over other beautiful hotels such as the Mont Fébé, Njeuga Palace, Hôtel des Députés, just to name these.

After checking into the hotel and placing their luggage in their room on the 11th floor, Joey called George, whose room was on the 10th floor, to tell him to join him and Emily at Le Panoramique, an impressive bar on the same floor as theirs.

The huge, bright windows of the bar offered a gorgeous panoramic view of the capital city. They spent over two hours taking in the beautiful sights outside the window while drinking local beer and snacking on sandwiches. From time to time, Emily could be seen tapping her feet and dancing in her seat to "Battoh" and "Wala Longo'o" by Petit Pays.

The next day was reserved for a visit to the campus of the University of Yaounde I, Joey's alma mater, where he obtained both his bachelors' and master' degrees. On their way to the institution, they stopped at Olezoa to see the approximately 23-foot-tall, spiral Reunification Monument. Constructed between 1973 and 1976, it was intended to memorialize the post-colonial marriage between British and French Cameroon, a corrosive union whose dirty, stinking laundry was swelling so precariously that it was just a matter of time before it would explode and throw its future into absolute uncertainty, unless intentional, honest, carefully targeted reforms were carried out by the government to stem the tide.

Emily and Joey went up the steps situated at the entrance of the symbol of the incredibly fragile unity of Anglophone and Francophone Cameroon and stood at the base of the gigantic, concrete structure for a few minutes while George took several pictures of them with his phone and the astounded American's Sony full-frame mirrorless digital camera. Then they took the internal steps that led to the tip of the spiral in circular fashion.

The top of the imposing monument gave a breathtaking view over the statue that sat proudly in front of the steps leading to the base. It was the statue of an old man carrying five children on both sides, on his back and on his lap. The toddlers clung to him tightly as he proudly waved the symbol of freedom, the national torch. The architects of the monument intended for the statue of the old man and the children to represent the former illuminating the path from the past, the ancestors, to the future, the younger generations.

From the tip of the monument, which took 53 tons of concrete to build and was actually a representation of two serpents spiraling with their heads merged at the top, a symbol of the two colonies that came together to form one, indivisible nation on October 1, 1961, the tourists also had magnificent panoramic views of Yaounde in all its splendor. They could see the beautiful buildings, the tall trees of various types, the municipal lake, the seven hills that surrounded the city, and lots more with stunning clarity. When they were completely drenched in the spectacular views that the summit of the monument offered, they decided to descend in order to continue their journey.

"If only an iota of the thoughtfulness and the vision of the creators of this Reunification Monument was replicated by the leaders of this nation, the country and its citizens would be so prosperous," Joey lamented as they drove away from the touristic attraction.

At the main campus of the University of Yaounde I in Ngoa Ekele, they toured all the buildings, starting with those housing the Department of English where he still had friends, some of whom had recently joined the faculty, and ending with the science buildings farther down the hill. Built mostly with black stones, cinder blocks, and concrete in 1962, the mother of the universities in the nation was made up of the Faculty of Arts, Letters and Social Sciences, the Faculty of Science, the Faculty of Medicine and Biomedical Sciences, the National Advanced School of Engineering, and the Higher Teachers' Training College.

At the end of their tour, which lasted almost two hours, they sat down at the "champignons" or the mushrooms, an on-campus, outdoor eatery consisting of several mushroom-shaped structures. An old friend, Albert, met them there.

"It's such a great pleasure to see you again, Joey, after four years," Albert said.

"Yes, it's been quite a while, bro, and I'm very happy to see you. Congratulations on your recruitment with the Department of English. I'm very sure that you're already leaving a mark as an impressive professor of practical English grammar."

"Thank you! So, who's this uniquely pretty lady who's glued to your side?"

"Oh, I'm sorry for not doing the introductions. This is my sweetheart, Emily and he is George, our resourceful driver who's been everywhere with us since we arrived in Cameroon. Emily, George, meet Albert, my classmate from undergrad all the way to graduate school on this campus."

They had a few beers, Satzenbrau to be exact, Joey's choice back in the day. Joey also had Emily try another of his favorite snacks from back then, cow liver stew with bread. She liked it, a lot. As the four of them ate and drank, they chatted about the changes that had taken place and were still occurring on campus. Buildings were receiving fresh coats of paint while pavements and other infrastructure were being repaired. New structures were also being erected.

When the two friends were done catching up, the tourists headed back downtown for their lunch reservation at Dolce Vita, across from the once popular but recently closed *Cinéma Abbia*. The restaurant was full that afternoon. Joey and Emily had pasta and grilled chicken while their driver was excited to try a hamburger the first time in his life. It was a super large hamburger, almost the size of a plate. By the time George was done eating, long before his companions, he had ketchup and mustard all over his face and on his shirt, like a three-year-old. It was obvious that he did not regret his choice.

"What do you think about the hamburger?" Emily teased.

"It's amazing! I think I'll get another one," he responded.

They retired to the Hilton around 4 pm and spent the evening relaxing. Emily called her parents at 5 pm, midnight in Delaware, as she had been doing daily since arriving in Cameroon, to update them about her stay in her boyfriend's country.

The rest of their trip to Yaounde involved touring the campus of the second state university, the University of Yaounde II in Soa, shopping for designer brands at floor level prices at *Marché Central,* purchasing traditional Cameroonian outfits and pieces of art for Emily and her family at Marché Mokolo, savoring grilled beef, locally called suya, at Briqueterie, appreciating artwork from all over Cameroon at the historic National Museum, visiting the National Assembly and the military headquarters in Ngoa Ekele, feeding animals at the zoo in Melen, exploring the impressive and majestic Yaounde Conference Center, and getting as close as permitted to the Unity Palace, the residence of the country's autocratic leader who had been in power for three decades thanks to constitutional modifications, election rigging, and brutalizing and jailing of opposition figures. They also made sure to dine at many of the numerous remarkable restaurants in the capital and to have a good time at some of the local nightclubs that Joey frequented back in the day, including Balafon, Katios, and Oxygène.

After an incredibly memorable stay in Yaounde, it was time to return to Mbengwi. They chose to take a different route from the previous one in order for Emily to see more of the country. Thus, they exited Yaounde via Etoudi and headed towards Obala, Bafia, and Makenene, a popular midpoint and resting spot. Unlike rest areas in the United States, where travelers stop to use the restroom and, perhaps, get a snack or a drink from a vending machine, Makenene had more than a dozen bars, restaurants, shops, an open-air market, and many more things for drivers and passengers.

The trio sat in one of the bars on the left side of the road for drinks. They also placed an order for fresh roasted corn on the cob and safou fruit, locally called plums, cooked on the grill.

"These are so yummy," Emily said of the safou. "Can we order some to-go to snack on later down the road?" she asked.

"Of course! George, please tell the lady to make some more

for the road," Joey requested.

Before resuming their travel, Joey filled a couple of bags with some food items that he knew his parents and siblings would appreciate, such as yams, potatoes, baguettes, wrapped fermented cassava roots, commonly known as bobolo (a perfect side for either ndole or beans), pineapples, oranges, and some more safou, not grilled though.

A couple of cities down the highway and they were out of the Central Region of which Yaounde was also the capital. They entered the West Region, the last Francophone province, and after driving through its main cities like Bandjoun, Bafoussam, and Mbouda, they were out of Francophone Cameroon, cruising deeper and deeper into the familiar terrain of the Northwest Region.

One knew one was entering the Anglophone province when the highway suddenly went from somewhat smooth to terrible, almost impassible, due to huge potholes in the tarred areas, and thick, gluelike mud in the parts of the road that were not paved. That route was like a cemetery for automobiles as many would break down from over exertion. Very often, inexperienced and frustrated drivers would give up and abandon their vehicles in the deep mud and walk away.

As the travelers approached Santa, one of the gateway cities into the Northwest, scores of Caterpillar dozers, graders, loaders, asphalt pavers, compactors, trucks, excavators, road reclaimers, and other pieces of road construction equipment could be seen rusting in disuse on both sides of the road. Plants were growing on some of them, an indication that they had been sitting there for quite a long time. Joey later found out that the equipment had been abandoned there for at least two years.

In fact, a company had received money from the government to tar the road from the entrance into the region all the way to the capital city, Bamenda, but the contractor had deserted the job after a few weeks without refunding a dime of the millions he had been given. Such an occurrence was not uncommon in Cameroon, especially in the English-speaking regions as companies felt very comfortable obtaining contracts from the government through kickbacks and abandoning the job as soon as payment was received. It was a mutually enriching scheme between contactors and corrupt government officials. The contractor would pocket a ton of cash, the official who awarded him or her the contact would get his cut, the job would not be done, and the poor citizens would be left to live without what they were promised by unscrupulous politicians. Meanwhile, it would be entered into official government records that the job was perfectly executed, completed, inspected, and inaugurated.

Luckily for George and his tired passengers, when his Toyota Camry got stuck in the mud, four strong guys appeared from one of the sundried brick houses on the side of the highway and offered to push it out if he would pay them 4,000 francs, about $8. The four shirtless men pushed the sedan in the thick mud down the road for about a mile until they made it to an old patch of pavement where George gave a little gas and freed the captive vehicle. Joey handed their rescuers 10,000 francs for their vigorous work and they continued their journey down the remaining partly passable and partly treacherous highway to Bamenda and onward to Mbengwi. While he was happy to be back on the way home to his family, he was troubled by the state of deterioration of the road, a sign of the neglect of the people by the government. He imagined the frustration every user of the road had to feel, and that made him worry about the future of the region.

Time has a way of flying when one is having the best time of one's life. That's exactly what happened during the remaining two weeks of Joey and Emily's stay in Cameroon. From a special church service requested by Joey's parents to thank God for abundant blessings on their family and to pray for his continuous guidance and protection, to trips to neighboring towns and villages like Bome, Njindom, Ngienbo, Nyen, Tad, Acha, Oshie, and Ngie, to family game and movie nights, to hiking in Abbi Falls, to hanging out with old friends and making new ones, and to romantic dates out of town to spend quality time together, their days were loaded with incredibly fun activities.

When the time came to depart, it was a bittersweet moment. Emily and Joey were tremendously appreciative of his family, especially his parents, for sparing nothing to make their vacation extremely amazing and refreshing. They were also pleased to be returning to the United States where they would spend about a month together before the familiar grit and grind resumed in August.

However, as Joey was packing his suitcase, he couldn't stop thinking about the ticking time bomb that the Anglophone region of Cameroon had become due to the marginalization and oppression of the citizens. The predominantly Francophone government, pejoratively referred to in the region as the government of La République to highlight the fact that it did not represent the interests of the English-speaking citizens and territories, had rendered the living conditions in the nation unbearable for the Anglophones and the latter had already proven that that they wouldn't hesitate to take their anger and frustrations out on anyone or anything that was remotely linked to Francophone Cameroon, even by name or origin. Before he was forced by circumstances to flee Cameroon in 2009, things were already bad, but in the short time that he had been in the United States, they had gotten dangerously precarious. Thus, he was debilitatingly worried about the future of his country. "What would happen to my family if, as the lady said at Mbon Market a few weeks ago, a war for Anglophone Cameroon's secession and independence broke out?" he wondered. What he had seen in the four weeks since returning home had only added credence to the likelihood of such a conflict occurring at some point in the near future, unless heaven intervened. "God help us; Lord, please protect my loved ones!" he let out, visibly scared.

With all the luggage loaded into the sedan and all departure checks completed, he sat down with his parents and poured his heart out. Everyone shared his worry about the troubling trajectory of the country, but they disagreed with him that their lives would be in danger simply because they were considered Francophones in the region.

"We've been here for more than 40 years. Mbengwi is our home; it's your home, Joey! We're Meta people now, and everyone in this town knows that," his father said as reassuringly as he could.

"Don't worry, JJ. We're going to be fine. Nobody would bother us if something like that happened," his mother added as she spread her arms for the longest motherly hug he could remember.

The faith and hopefulness of his parents allayed his worries slightly. After prolonged hugs and kisses with his parents and siblings, Joey and Emily finally left Mbengwi at 9:15 am on June 30th to catch an evening flight bound for Brussels from the Douala International Airport.

CHAPTER TEN

MILESTONES

2013 opened with a lot of hope and promise for Joey. It looked like a year that would fill his life with beautiful sunshine and roses. The first in a series of exciting happenings was the word that he received from his dissertation committee president in early January that his research on effective discipline of intellectually advanced high school students in five local public schools had been approved for defense, unanimously. That was phenomenal news as he had burned the midnight candle, for several months, revising and editing chapters of his work at the request of unsatisfied committee members.

On at least two occasions in December of 2012 alone, one of the professors requested changes on pieces of the dissertation that had been given the green light by all of the other colleagues on the committee. On another occasion, when he was at the end of the dissertation process, a different member suddenly sent him back to take out whole sections of the first chapter that everyone, including him, had approved months earlier. It was incredibly shocking and frustrating for Joey, and he was in the middle of drafting an angry email calling out the inconsistencies and confusion of the professor when Emily warned, "Don't poke the bear, honey. The guy probably didn't read the chapter when he okayed it the first time, and rather than letting you move forward with something that he thought had room for improvement, he wanted you to make the improvements before progressing. So, just do whatever he's telling you to do, and everything will be just fine, babe. You've worked so hard on this, and I'm immensely proud of you, future Dr. Jumessi!"

Therefore, the news from the committee chair was the fruit of his monumental patience and consistent hard work.

In order to fulfill the requirements to participate in the May 11th commencement ceremony, he needed to accept a defense date that was no later than the end of February. He accepted the date that the committee had agreed upon, February 20th. He immediately sprang into action to ensure that his students would have a highly qualified substitute teacher and meaningful work to do in his absence on that day.

With two important events already set in stone, Joey thought about adding another one, an even bigger and enormously important one, to the list. It was something that he had been considering carefully for more than three years. The time had come to take the relationship with the love of his life to the next level, he thought. It would be great if he could ask her to marry him on the day of his graduation. That way, both his and her parents and, if possible, his siblings would witness him dropping the knee.

A feat like that would require meticulous planning in addition to a significant amount of money to get his parents and siblings to the United States in such a short time. Worst case scenario, he could make arrangements for just his parents to travel. His mind was racing; all the thoughts were ringing joyful bells in his head.

He called his father on January 12th, a day after he found out about the defense and graduation, to tell him what he was thinking about pulling off in less than five months.

"That's a lot to do in such a short time, and it would cost a lot of money, although it would be worth every penny," his father advised.

"I think so too. If everybody can't come, at least you and Mami should be here to see me graduate and ask Emily to marry me," Joey requested.

"Absolutely! I'll see what I could do to help. I'm very proud of you, Joey!"

"Thank you, Papa! I will send you all the documents that you and Mami would need to take to the US Embassy to apply for your visas."

"Awesome! Keep us posted."

When he got off the phone with his father, he called Mr. Goldman to announce his upcoming dissertation defense and graduation and to invite him and his wife to the May 11th commencement ceremony. Additionally, and most importantly, the phone call was to officially discuss with Emily's father his intention to ask his daughter's hand in marriage. When the thought of marrying Emily first crossed his mind many months prior, he saw the conversation with her parents occurring face-to-face, but given the fact that a unique opportunity had come up to make the event even more exciting and memorable, he needed to act fast to get everything lined up for a May engagement.

Mr. Goldman answered the call, and after pleasantries, Joey got to the purpose for reaching out. He laid out everything he wanted to do and apologized for not meeting him in person for the once-in-a-lifetime request.

"Oh wow! That's wonderful! That's amazing! You have my blessings, and I am sure my wife's too," Mr. Goldman responded with infantile elation.

"I'm deeply sorry again for not meeting you face-to-face for this extremely important request. I just thought that the timing would be perfect to ask Emily to marry me in front my parents and you and in the presence of our friends."

"Nothing to apologize for, son. This is a very huge deal, and I agree with you that the timing is perfect. If there's anything you need to make this day greater than it already sounds, just ask me, okay! Straight off the top of my head, I already know that I would like to pay for the graduation party."

"Thank you very much, Mr. Goldman. Thank you so much!"

With the parents thus notified, Joey went shopping for an affordable yet befitting engagement ring at the Greenville mall. After looking at multiple pieces in different stores, his sight landed on a gorgeous emerald cut diamond ring that was on sale for $4,999.00.

"That's a fabulous ring. She's going to be ecstatic," the female store attendant/jewelry specialist said.

"I think she would. It's a beautiful ring. I would give her one with a bigger rock on it, if I could afford it, but I think she would be very happy with this one."

"You can always upgrade later, on your anniversary, for instance," the lady suggested

Joey left the mall satisfied with the choice he had made, and on his way home, he played all the upcoming events in his head with enormous anticipation.

The day of the terminal degree culminating task came fast. Emily, who had taken the day off from law school to support her man, drove him to the campus of Delta State University, and they arrived one hour ahead of the 10:00 am defense. They walked to the second floor of the building that housed the school of education and sat in the lounge area.

"You got this, babe. Relax!" she encouraged him when she felt the palpable nervousness that was emanating from him.

He had so much self-confidence in the days leading up to the academic exercise and even during the ride to Cleveland that morning, but as soon as they made it to the DSU campus, the reality and the weight of what he was about to do hit him suddenly. In just a few hours, he would permanently shed off the Mr. in front of his name in favor of the more dignifying, hard-earned Dr., and the more he thought about what that would mean to him, his family, his friends, and, of course, his sweetheart, the more nervous he became.

At exactly 9:55 am, his advisor, came out of the conference

room and walked towards them.

"Good morning, Joey! Are you ready?" Dr. Bradshaw asked.

"Yes, sir!"

Joey introduced his girlfriend to the professor who was visibly surprised by his discovery of the biracial couple. Professor Bradshaw then went over the defense expectations and procedures with his candidate and announced, to Joey's chagrin, that guests were not allowed in the room during the culminating terminal degree task.

"That's fine. I'll just wait right here," Emily said, trying to hide her disappointment.

She hugged him tightly as she whispered in his ear, "You got this, Dr. Jumessi!" Then she kissed him.

Joey walked into the conference room with regained confidence. His committee chair sat at the far end of the 12-seat meeting table, while two members sat to his right and the remaining duo occupied the seats directly across from them. After greetings and introductions and a few words intended to dispel any anxiety or nervousness that the candidate might feel, Joey was instructed to use the equipment located at the other end of the massive cherry table for his PowerPoint presentation.

He used all the time allotted to present a summary of his research. His tongue was tight during the first five minutes of his presentation, but he quickly regained the confidence and the fluidity and fluency of thought and expression that he was known to have. Following the synopsis was questioning, and that went on for more than two hours. He answered each of the questions with great command and effectiveness. Then, suddenly, no one had anything else that he or she needed to inquire about the study, and the researcher was told to wait in the hallway while the committee deliberated.

The grilling had worn him out, so he was very pleased to hear that it was over. He felt like a heavy weight had been lifted off his shoulders as he walked out of the room.

"How did it go, babe?" yelled Emily as she scurried towards Joey as soon as she saw him.

"I think I did a great job. They sent me out here to wait while they decide my fate."

"You see! I told you that you would do well."

"You sure did, honey. I just got a little nervous when we got here this morning. But I'm glad it's over now."

They walked back to the lounge area, but before they could sit down, he was summoned back to the room for the results.

Every member of the dissertation committee, starting with the president, congratulated him on exceptional research and a brilliantly written and defended dissertation. They shook his hand as he thanked each of them for their guidance and support all through the dissertation journey. Emily was allowed into the room for the results phase, and he introduced her to the professors. She pulled out her camera and took scores of pictures to memorialize the monumental event.

After driving off the Cleveland campus, Joey and Emily went to a Mexican restaurant across from Walmart to celebrate.

"I'm glad the weight is off my shoulders now," he said as he cut a juicy piece of Steak Ranchero. He had done something that he had thought about many years earlier in Cameroon. Back then, pursuing a doctorate was just an impossible dream because of his circumstances. He was struggling financially and worries about his future did not allow him the mental fortitude that such a mighty pursuit required. Therefore, he was incredibly proud of himself and thankful to God for making what was once impossible a reality.

"You did it, JJ! I'm so proud of you. When is graduation? Has it been scheduled yet?"

"Yes, it's going to be on May 11th."

"That's in two months. What would you like to do after the

commencement ceremony? It would be great if your parents could come. We could have a small celebration and invite your CAMSUS friends and some of your colleagues. What do you think, honey?"

Her thoughts aligned very closely with the plans that he had already set in motion, but he did not want her to know about them, as he wanted everything to be a surprise to her.

"I think those are good ideas, but I am not sure I want to be with anyone else but you on the day of my graduation. I was thinking we could go somewhere, maybe to Nashville, after the commencement ceremony. We could spend the weekend there, have a really good time, just you and me."

"If that's what you want, then that's what we will do, babe. It's your special day that you have worked extremely hard for. So, we'll do exactly what you want."

For the first time in all the years they had been together, he was dissembling. He wanted to tell her about the plans that were already taking shape behind her back, from his parents arriving on May 10th, to her father funding a huge celebration at the Marriott in downtown Memphis, and to his and her friends being invited to what was hoped to be a spectacular celebration of academic accomplishment and love, but he just could not tell her about all those things without hinting at the engagement. Thus, in order not to mess up everything, he was hiding everything from her, such a heavy burden to carry for more than two months.

For the next two months, everything proceeded mostly as planned. Joey's siblings were not granted visas to enter the United States with the bogus reason that the embassy did not think that they would return to Cameroon. Only his parents were allowed to travel. Invitations were sent out to friends with the warning not to disclose to Emily. Joey drove to Memphis a couple of times to meet with the staff of the hotel in charge of planning the celebration. Mr. Goldman had pretty much written him a blank check for the event, and he was determined to make sure that everything would be nice, not exaggerated, just enough for every guest to have a really good time.

All the plans were concluded by May 1st, and everything was set for a celebration filled with surprises.

On Friday, May 10th, Joey secretly picked up his parents from the Memphis International Airport. He had already outlined the plans to them, so they were not surprised that Emily did not show up to welcome them. He drove them to the Marriott where they would stay until May 12th. After having dinner with them and making sure that they settled comfortably in the room, he went over to his girlfriend's house to spend the night.

The next morning, both he and Emily left for Cleveland at 6:30 and arrived at 9:00 o'clock. The Coliseum, the venue of the commencement, was already filling up very fast. Joey alighted from the car, took his robe from a suit bag and wore it over his black suit. The black robe with black velvet lining on both sides of the long top-down zipper fit him just right, neither loose nor tight. The triple black velvet stripes on the exterior of each sleeve, each representing the bachelor's, master's and doctoral degrees, were pride-provoking. He looked at them with a broad smile of joy.

"You look great, babe. Let me take a picture of you and text it to my parents and to your mom and dad. They're going to be so proud! I hate that they're missing such a milestone moment," Emily said with mixed emotions.

He posed for a few pictures, trying really hard to hide from her the fact that her parents were on a flight to Memphis as she was taking the shots.

He found a good seat in the bleachers for Emily, before joining the rest of the graduates who were lining up outside to get ready for the procession into the Coliseum.

The commencement ceremony started on time. Three

graduates, all male, were getting a doctorate at the ceremony. 55 others were getting a master's degree, while the rest of the recipients, 275 of them, were graduating with a bachelor's degree. Joey led the procession of graduates into the Coliseum, and, as soon as he appeared at the entrance, marching to the tune of "Pomp and Circumstance," played by the school's band, there was loud cheering, chanting, and screams. One of the voices he could hear, probably the loudest on his left, was one that he knew too well, that of his greatest cheerleader. She was clapping, screaming, and blowing kisses, making it very clear to everyone that she had a dear one graduating. He waved at her and blew a few kisses in reciprocation.

After all the ceremonial speeches, the long-awaited moment came for the award of diplomas, starting with doctoral degrees. Following the order of the entry procession, Joey Kemdong Jumessi Jr. was the first name called. He could hear Emily shouting her lungs out as he took the steps of the stage. He was greeted at the top by his dissertation advisor who proceeded to hooding him. A handshake and a congratulatory hug later, Joey was standing in front of the president of Delta State University, Dr. Laforge. Another handshake and a large green leather diploma cover with gold lettering was handed to him by the dean of the College of Education. That was it! What he had pursued so ferociously for four years, a diploma which at times seemed elusive, getting out of reach, was finally in his hands. Suddenly, a feeling he had never felt before, perhaps a spirit, took total control of him, and he found himself vigorously doing some Mukonge moves, a traditional dance from the Meta people in Mbengwi, where he was born, the place that he proudly called his hometown. Everyone in the Coliseum, from the families in the bleachers, to the dignitaries on stage, burst into applauses, even as he walked off, proudly raising his diploma in the air and blowing kisses to the beautiful White lady who was screaming at the top of her lungs.

At the end of the ceremony, they swung by his apartment

in Indianola to pack up a small luggage, enough for the weekend trip to Nashville that he had told her about. While in Indianola, he pretended to use the restroom, so that he could call to check on his parents and on Mr. and Mrs. Goldman. He also called the event planner to make sure that everything was going as planned. The guests, consisting of their friends and a few of his colleagues, were in on the plan, and they knew exactly when to report to the hotel and what to do while there.

They made it back to Memphis at 5:00 pm, and he suggested that they take a shower and get dressed in their best outfits so that they would hit the ground running as soon as they made it to Nashville. She put on a gorgeous blue Chanel dress with a long posterior zipper and a pair of blue Gucci platform sandals. She looked stunningly pretty. On his part, he put on a dark gray suit with a white shirt, a blue tie that matched her dress and a pair of black shoes. A couple of sprays of his Aqua di Giò fragrance by Giorgio Armani and he was ready to go. It was 7:15 pm. "It's going to be 11:00 pm when we make it to Nashville," she warned.

"I know. That's why I wanted us to get dressed before leaving so that we could go straight to the club when we get there. However, before we leave, I need us to stop at the Marriott downtown to pick up a graduation present from one of my friends who is in Memphis for a conference."

One of Joey's friends, a member of CAMSUS, met him at the lobby of the hotel when they arrived, and as planned, he suggested that they sit down somewhere for dinner to celebrate the graduation. Emily gave Joey a look of frustration as she knew that they were going to be running late getting to Nashville, but she decided to follow her man, as they walked down a hallway, she not suspecting anything, until they got to the double doors leading to the banquet hall, and she recognized her former roommates in Indianola and other friends of Joey's as soon as the doorman flung the doors open.

"What's going on here? What are my roommates and all

these other people doing here?" she asked, absolutely surprised.

The event planner, Miss Fisher, responded, "Welcome to Dr. Jumessi's graduation party!"

"I'll kill you, JJ!" she yelled, feigning to punch him in his face. "I thought you said you did not want to party," she added.

The MC declared the celebration officially started with the celebrant's entry into the hall, and there were cheers, chants, and screams as Joey and his girlfriend were escorted to the special table. 100 guests honored the invitation, and they were seated five per table in the hall. At the far end of the room, directly across from the double doors, was an infinite spread of all types of food, wine, spirits, beer, and punch. Servers, sharply dressed in black bottoms and white tops with bowties, were ensuring that plates and glasses stayed permanently replenished with hors d'oeuvres and drinks respectively.

Then, about 20 minutes after their arrival, Joey's phone dinged, and he pulled it out of his breast pocket and leaned away from Emily to read what the screen said. When he was done, he gestured for the MC to come over.

"I would like to say something before we continue," he told the MC who in turn asked for everyone's attention and handed the microphone to Joey who went and stood in the empty space reserved for dancing in the middle of the hall.

"Thank you all for taking time out of your hectic schedules to come out tonight to celebrate with me. I really appreciate you from the bottom of my heart. As some of you already know, a doctoral program could be overwhelmingly stressful, frustrating, and exhausting, requiring a tremendous degree of patience, perseverance, and resilience. There were times when I wanted to give up, but thanks to a formidable support system surrounding me, I was able to bulldoze my way through and make it to the finish line. I would like to thank you, my friends, for your consistent encouragement during my time at Delta State. To my colleagues at Gentry, who stepped up sometimes

to cover for me at the last minute when I had to run to DSU for some unpredictable matters that came up, I am forever indebted to you. My parents taught me the value of hard work and the importance of clinging to set goals, even when things are tough, like they very often were in my doctoral program. I love them dearly and appreciate them for imparting these valuable lessons to me and my siblings. And, finally, to my exceptional lady, Emily, who has been by my side since my first days in the United States, I say I couldn't have done this without you. She has accompanied me through thick and thin, often making sacrifices that very few people would just to be with me. There were times when I was ready to throw in the towel, but she was there to support and encourage me to keep fighting. I remember this one time when one of my committee members told me to redo something that he had already approved several months earlier, and I was so mad that I got my computer and started typing an email to call out and cuss the professor, but she caught me in time and talked some sense into my head. She knows how to calm me down when I am frustrated or angry. In fact, she knows everything about me. She is the perfect woman for me, a keeper and that's why..."
At that time, the double doors swung open again, and revealed a couple in their sixties, dressed in Afritude, traditional Cameroonian regalia. They were holding a long banner between them, and they walked slowly towards their son as he was getting on one knee. The words on the beautifully decorated banner read, "Will you be my partner for life? Will you marry me, Emily?"

The person sitting next to Emily, one of her friends, caught her on time before she hit the ground as she fell off her seat. What she was witnessing was tremendously overwhelming to her. She had not even gotten over the surprise graduation party, then the man of her dreams was asking her to marry him. Then, Joey's parents, who she last saw in June of 2012, were physically standing in front of her. Rendering the surprise even more incredible, standing right behind the bearers of the marriage proposal, were Mr. and Mrs. Goldman, her parents.

Supported by the friend who caught her from falling, she walked to the center of the room, a river flowing from her eyes. Overwhelmed with joy, she collapsed into Joey's arms, while he was still down on one knee, prompting the audience, who were in total euphoria, to chant in unison, "Answer! Answer! Answer! Answer!"

She regained some consciousness at that time and answered, "Yes, I'll marry you, JJ," as loudly as she could, to the applause of everyone in the banquet hall. Joey pulled the ring out of its black box, reached for her left hand, and gently slid the diamond jewelry down the fourth finger from the thumb. Even the parents were carried away by emotions at that moment.

The atmosphere in the room was magical. It was hard for the audience to recover from the emotions caused by the fantastic scene that had unfolded in front of them, and while people were taking pictures and calling friends and family on their cell phones to describe the unbelievable show that they had witnessed, Joey grabbed the mic again to thank his soon-to-be-parents-in-law for their support, generosity, and the guidance.

The newly engaged couple was solicited at times individually and at other times together by guests for a dance or pictures or a chat or all three for hours. The newly met soon-to-be-parents-in-law seemed to get along pretty well all night, after having spent most of the day together at the hotel. At one point in the night, Joey looked over to check on his parents and he saw his mother teaching Mr. Goldman how to dance Coupé Décalé, while Mrs. Goldman and his father were dancing together less than a foot from them. It was a beautiful sight to see. Two White parents, who just three years earlier where against their only daughter dating a Black man, were happily celebrating her engagement to that Black guy. "The stone that the builders had rejected, had become the cornerstone," Joey thought as he was dancing with his fiancée. The Goldmans, especially Mrs. Goldman, were resting the future of their family on him and Emily, and he was determined to make them and his parents proud.

He decided that night, on that dance floor, that he could not afford to live a day away from Emily anymore. "I'm going to start looking for a job in Memphis, so that we won't have to be apart anymore," he whispered in her ear.

"That would be great, honey! I was already thinking about moving to Indianola to be with you, and drive two hours 30 minutes to Memphis, three times per week, until I finish school next year."

"You won't have to do that, babe. I'm moving to Memphis."

After breakfast the next morning, Joey and Emily give a tour of Memphis to their parents. They took them to see the home of Elvis Presley at Graceland. After that, they went to the world-famous Memphis Zoo to see exotic animals. In the afternoon, they went shopping at Wolfchase Mall and from there they returned to the hotel to drop off all the items they had bought before going to Rendezvous, the famous barbecue restaurant on Beale Street, for dinner.

Very early on Monday morning, Emily drove her parents to the airport, before her first period class, while Joey and his parents departed for Indianola. When they made it to Cleveland, he detoured to DSU to show his parents the school he had attended for over three years. The drive around the campus lasted about 20 minutes, and they were back on Hwy 61, heading to Sunflower County.

As soon as he returned home, Joey started applying for teaching positions in Memphis. He could not apply for administrative positions yet because he still had to take the school leadership licensure exam in order to become certified. He did not hear anything about the 20 applications that he sent to public and private schools in Shelby County for the remaining 12 days of the school year, but on Friday, May 31st, the day before his parents had to return to Cameroon, he received an email from the principal of a high school located in Arlington, TN, about 25 minutes out of Memphis. He called the school leader at the number provided and arranged to go in for an interview at 9:00 am on June 3rd.

The school district, Shelby County Schools, paid significantly better than the system he worked for in Indianola. With his doctoral degree and years of experience, he could see a tremendous spike in his pay if he got hired. He could be able to afford a house and, perhaps, a new car to replace the beat-up Nissan he had.

At the airport on Saturday, June 1st, no tears were shed like when he and Emily were leaving Mbengwi a year earlier. His parents were very happy about the fact that they had witnessed their son's remarkable achievements. Upon leaving Cameroon, they thought that they were going to his graduation, but their trip was made even more thrilling by his memorable engagement to Emily. They witnessed an amazing bonus milestone, something that they had been secretly praying for because they wanted her to become a part of their family one day.

"We'll be seeing both of you again very soon at the wedding when we schedule it," Joey told his parents as he gave them a goodbye hug.

"Absolutely! Take your time to plan everything before scheduling the ceremony, but you don't want to wait too long," his father advised. His mother nodded her head in agreement.

"We'll do it when we're ready," Emily said, smiling and as she held Joey's mother's right hand with both of hers.

"Thank you both for an amazing time; we had fun seeing places and trying different cuisines in the Mississippi Delta, Jackson, Biloxi and here in Memphis," Joey's mother said.

"You're welcome. We'll do even more next time," said

Emily as the parents hugged their son and daughter-in-law-to-be again before heading towards security check.

Upon returning to Emily's apartment, Joey sat at the desktop to do some research about Bolton High School, the school he was going to for an interview on Monday morning. In addition to being up-to-date with content knowledge, instructional best practices, classroom management, etc., he needed to make sure that he knew as much as possible about the school and the community. When he was done preparing for the interview, he printed out the directions to the school.

He reported for his appointment 10 minutes early, and the secretary had him wait in the conference room. Before long the principal, a guidance counselor, and the head of the English Department filed into the room and introduced themselves. After brief pleasantries to make the candidate comfortable, the interview began. He impressed everyone with his expansive knowledge of the high school English and French curricula and effective instructional practices. He spoke about their school like he had spent a long time there, and as a result of the effectiveness of his answers to the questions, he was offered the job on the spot. Just like at Gentry, he would be teaching both English and French to juniors.

Before leaving the campus, he texted Emily the good news. He knew she was in class and did not want to disturb her with a phone call, although she would not have minded. She called him a short time later.

"Congratulations, babe! I'm so proud of you, you just don't know how excited I am right now."

They spent the rest of the summer together at her apartment, and two weeks before school started, in August, they both went down to Indianola to vacate his place. Although he had been preparing for his new job all summer, he intensified his readiness the week before school resumed. He borrowed the textbooks for both courses from the school and read them along with the curriculum maps and other resources that he downloaded from the school district's website. He also bought classroom supplies, including posters, markers, staplers, pens, pencils, pencil sharpeners, erasers, and other items that he thought he would need for at least the first week of school. He was ready to make an immensely positive impression on his first day at Bolton high school.

CHAPTER ELEVEN

AN INCREDIBLE FIRST WEEK

As soon as the parent-teacher meetings were over, Joey called Emily, as he was heading to the parking lot, to talk about the incredible day he had.

"You wouldn't believe what happened today," he said.

"What happened, babe? You didn't get in trouble, did you?"

"No, not at all!"

He told her everything, starting with the slur that he discovered on the wall in his classroom, how he was more shocked that someone could write something on the wall without him noticing than about the vile words themselves. He recounted how he was planning to investigate the matter, to unmask the hand that wrote the "Go back to Africa!" comment and how the mystery was burst wide open accidentally by a couple who came to the parent-teacher meetings.

"That's crazy. How did the parents react when they found out that their son was the person who wrote the slur?"

"They were very surprised. They said that they were not racist and that their son knew better. They cried and apologized on behalf of their son. They also said that he would be apologizing the first thing tomorrow morning."

"Does the kid look like the type of person who would do something like that? I mean, has he given you any reasons in the four days that you have been teaching at Bolton to even watch him closely?"

"Not really. He's just a very talkative fellow; that's all."

"You know, babe, this does not surprise me at all. When you told me on Monday about the demographic makeup of the students and the faculty and staff of your school, something told me that it won't be long before racist and xenophobic acts and comments start landing. The good thing is that you are better equipped to handle all of that now than you were when you dealt with things like these when you started teaching in Indianola four years ago."

"Absolutely! It's clear to me that I will be dealing with these things everywhere I go in this country. That's why I'm thinking about raising awareness among my students about racial and ethnic diversity. I plan on assigning a reflection exercise like what I did with my students in Indianola."

"That would help them learn about other countries, cultures, and people, which in turn would make them more informed and more respectful of people who don't look, sound, or behave like them," Emily remarked.

The next day Justin did not apologize like his parents had promised. Instead, he acted like everything was fine. During the last 20 minutes of first period, Dr. Jumessi told the class about an additional assignment that would be done twice a month. He had each student pick a country on any continent, excluding North America. He was surprised to find out that 99% of the class could not name any countries in the world, apart from the United States, Canada, and Mexico. Many of them thought Africa and Europe were countries. It was unbelievable that the students had made it to the 11th grade without knowing much about anything beyond the borders of the United States. As a result, and to his advantage, he started naming mostly countries that were in Africa and the Caribbean. Once each of the 25 students in the class had chosen a country, he distributed the directions of the assignment, the rubric, and several exemplars from his students at Gentry.

He explained to the class that the assignment would enhance their researching, writing, and reflecting skills as well as their knowledge of other countries and cultures. Almost everyone loved the assignment, except for three students among whom was the boy sitting under the hateful comment, the same student whose writing had prompted the teacher to assign the current event summary and reflection project to all the classes that he taught.

"Why don't you like the assignment, Justin?" Dr. Jumessi asked.

"What does this have to do with English? I just feel like it's punishment for what I wrote on the wall," he responded. His response got everyone's attention, and they wanted to see what he was talking about.

"First of all, I said that this project would enhance your researching, reading, and writing skills, all of which are fundamental aspects of the English III curriculum. And, yes, I believe that, if you were more aware of the people, cultures, and languages of the world, you would be less likely to write something as hateful as what you wrote above your head on that wall."

Justin did not say anything else, probably because he was embarrassed by the things that his peers were saying as they too read the slur.

"Why would you tell the teacher something like that, moron?" a peer yelled.

Others asked, "You thought people couldn't tell by your handwriting that you did that?"

Most of the students were disgusted by the comment and offered to erase it, but the teacher wanted it up there to serve as a testament to the hate and ignorance of at least one student at the school and a reminder of the importance of racial and ethnic awareness. Secretly, the teacher wanted it to torture the writer every time that he walked into his classroom.

Joey assigned the same project to his other five classes with the sole difference being that his French students were limited to the Francophone world. Word about the origin of the assignment had spread among the entire student body by lunchtime, such that students in his afternoon classes started asking questions about the work as soon as they walked into his classroom.

Just like love always trumps hate, by the end of that Friday, his fifth day at his new school, it was clear that condemnation of Justin's racist comment was widespread. The vast majority of the students he taught, and many that were not on his rosters, thought it important to let him know in the hallway that he was appreciated, loved, and highly respected.

On Monday of the following week, the principal's secretary called him to say that the principal needed him in his office during his planning period. He wondered what he might have done to be summoned to the main office. In all the years that he had been teaching in the United States, he had learned from colleagues that a call to the main office was not a good thing most of the time. Consequently, he started rolling back the tape of his first week in his mind to see what he might have done wrongly to warrant such a sudden request to report to the principal's office. He had done everything by the book, even coming in very early every day, working very hard and staying late after school to prepare his room and any materials that would be needed for the next day's classes.

Thus, feeling confident that he had not done anything inappropriate, he went to meet the principal, Mr. Overton, a tall overweight White man in his early sixties, who stood up from behind his desk and revealed his khaki pants below a navy-blue sport coat, white shirt, and tan tie. He told Joey to shut the door behind him, extended his hand for a handshake, and told him to have a seat. Joey sat in one of the two maroon chairs facing the principal's desk, feeling somewhat relieved that the mood was not ominous.

"How's your first week Dr. Jumessi?" Mr. Overton asked, smiling broadly.

"It was very productive. I liked the fact that my students

came in daily ready to learn, and that kept me on my toes from bell to bell every day.

"That's great! I've heard some great things about you from the students, and I want you to know that I've your back, we're here to support you, and we love you here at Bolton."

"Thank you, sir!" Joey said, wondering where the conversation was heading.

"I also heard about the situation with Justin, and I like the way you handled it, using it as an opportunity to raise awareness about diversity. However, there must be some consequences for him. He needs to be punished for disrespecting you and for vandalizing school property. Additionally, his parents need to know about what he did."

Joey told Mr. Overton how Justin's parents found out about the writing on the wall and their reaction.

"Did he apologize to you like his parents promised?"

"No Sir!"

"That means he's not remorseful; he does not regret what he did, and it's not acceptable! That behavior can't be tolerated. I'll handle it, I promise you! Go ahead and turn in a referral today, and let his parents know that he has not apologized for his racist, disrespectful language."

Mr. Overton went on to underscore his support for his new hire.

"We're a family here at Bolton. My team and I will always defend you when you are attacked or disrespected by anyone—colleagues, parents or students."

The administrator went on to cite an example of him standing up for his new teacher on the second day of school. He recounted to Joey how on the previous Tuesday he received phone calls from several parents asking that their child be removed from "that African's class." They asked why the administration of Bolton High School had an African teaching English to American kids. Even after he told the parents that Dr. Jumessi had advanced degrees in English and a doctoral degree in education in addition to being a level 5 teacher for the past four years, they still were not satisfied.

The principal's narrative shed more light on the origin of a rude remark that a student had made on Wednesday morning. Dr. Jumessi had corrected the kid who had used "every since" instead of "ever since" in a sentence. When he told her that she was wrong, she said, "How would you know? You're from Africa!" Many in the classroom burst out laughing as the teacher reached for a dictionary that he kept on his desk and handed it to another student to look for both phrases. Less than a minute later he yelled, "Every since does not exist. I found ever since, and it means 'from that time until now or continually.'" Everyone calmed down as the class continued. Dr. Jumessi kept his cool all along; He was used to being in situations that tested his patience.

Joey left Mr. Overton's office happy and appreciative of the full support pledged by his boss. He was not naive to think that his tenure at the high school would be without bumps, but as long as he had the administration by his side, no challenge would be insurmountable.

CHAPTER TWELVE

HERITAGE

By the end of the fall of 2013, Joey and Emily easily arrived at key decisions regarding the date and venue for their wedding. After discussing with their families, they settled on both a western style wedding and a traditional marriage ceremony as both would be in line with their values. Also, they concurred that Emily needed to be done with law school before the ceremonies in order to avoid distractions to her studies.

Therefore, the American style wedding would take place on Saturday July 19th, 2014, with a church service at the Catholic Church of Nativity in Bartlett followed by a reception at the Esplanade in Cordova. However, both events would be preceded on June 13th by a traditional Bamileke marriage rite that would be witnessed by a smaller group of invitees, mostly family and close friends. The latter event was a requirement among the Bamilike people of Dchang, where Joey's parents were born.

Although these decisions were not hard to make, they were not without hitches. For instance, more than three years after meeting Joey for the first time and leaving no doubts about their disdain for Black people and interracial relationships, Emily's grandparents slammed the door to an invitation to talk about their granddaughter's wedding. Mr. and Mrs. Goldman and their daughter were disappointed and hurt, although they pretended it was not a big deal. What bride would not want the blessings of her grandparents on her wedding, and be ecstatic that they were present to see her walk down the aisle?

Another insignificant issue, but nonetheless shocking, to both Joey and Emily, was the discovery that some of his Cameroonian "brothers" and "sisters" wondered why, with all the beautiful single Cameroonian women in the United States and back home, he chose to get married to an American.

While discussing this unsurprising issue with his best friend, John, one Sunday evening, the latter comically compared intermarriage to a party where there was an abundance of different types of food from around the world. He said, "Some invitees relished the ndole while others preferred the pasta as other guest filled up with the chimichanga. A few others liked the hibachi and sushi, just like many loved the steak, broccoli, and mashed potatoes. There were also some who gobbled the murg makhani, while the kung pao chicken got several people returning to the table for more. Similarly, some people loaded up on the thiep bou dien as many more savored the chimi churi. By the end of the event, do you know what the most exciting thing on everyone's mind was?"

"No!" Joey responded, intrigued.

"Everyone was very happy because they had eaten and drunk to their satisfaction. And that right there, my friend, is the most important thing about marriage. Marriage is all about what makes you happy; it's about what satisfies you. It has nothing to do with race, ethnicity, or religious background. There is no guarantee that a person would be happy and satisfied with a spouse from their own tribe or their home country."

John had a way of simplifying even the most complex things, with great humor too, and that was part of the glue that kept their friendship so tight.

Joey made sure to let those who were not in favor of his choice of a lifetime partner know that their opinions were irrelevant. Also, they would not receive an invitation to his wedding.

With law school off Emily's mind after her graduation in the spring of that year, preparations for the wedding intensified. There were lots of meetings with experts charged with different aspects of the celebration. If the couple was not needed to taste food samples and drinks, it would be something else like seating arrangements that had to be discussed, or the colors of the plates that needed to be reviewed, or pictures that had to be taken, or something else that their opinion was needed for planning.

Long hours were also spent on the phone with Joey's parents and grandparents to talk about documents needed for appointments at the American embassy in Yaounde for visas for them and his older sister. Both the future bride and groom were so surprised by how much time, effort, and money the wedding preparation was taking that they started anticipating the rest and relaxation that the honey-moon would provide.

The day of the big, American-style wedding ceremony arrived, finally. Joey was so happy that his parents and his older sister were present. Three of his groomsmen were classmates from college in Cameroon; they had immigrated to the United States after undergrad and had remained in touch with him. Another close friend, a former classmate from graduate school, was the fourth groomsman, while the remaining two were Andy and Josh, his roommates from his early days in the United States. They all looked very spiffy in their black tuxedos, white shirts, black bow ties, and black oxfords.

On her part, the bride had four of her cousins, Joey's older sister, and one of her colleagues at Spitzer and Sachs, a prominent law firm in Memphis, as her bridesmaids. They were clad in olive sleeveless dresses.

Standing at the altar, next to his best man, John, and the priest, Joey couldn't believe his eyes when the doors of the church opened and revealed his bride in an extremely beautiful white dress that accentuated her hourglass shape and had a seemingly endless train. Her diamond tiara set fittingly on her head like that of a royal. With her left arm interlocked in her father's right arm, she slowly and elegantly walked down the aisle, with enough radiance to light up the darkest place on earth. Mr. Goldman had never been seen as happy as he was for the few minutes he spent walking his only child down the aisle in his very elegant and stylish black tuxedo, white shirt and black bow tie. He had a similar outfit designed for his son-in-law by a famous suit maker in New York City.

The bride and the groom said their individually written vows in front of a huge audience made up of their families and close friends. They professed profound love and dedication for each other till the end of time. By the time they were done, it was impossible to find a dry cheek in the church. Even the priest reached into his pocket and pulled out a handkerchief to wipe a tear that snuck out of his right eye.

Immediately after the church service, which ended at 7:00 pm, everyone transitioned to the Esplanade, about 20 minutes away, for the splendid reception that lasted all night. There was so much to eat and drink from mostly the United States and Cameroon, that many guests and some of the waiters packed plenty to take home after the ceremony. The rest was carried to the newlyweds' apartment.

The solemnity and formality of the American wedding, especially the part in church, contrasted sharply with the relaxed, jovial nature of the traditional Bamileke marriage ceremony that took place in the event hall of Joey and Emily's apartment complex the previous evening. The bride and groom as well as their parents and Joey's sister were all clad in beautiful, multicolor outfits made from hand-embroidered, high quality, ethnic material called atoghu. While the females wore mini kabas, a type of dress, the males wore vests of similar fabric and colors, including blue, black, red, yellow, and white, with black pants. A special dress design and jewelry made from cowy shells clearly distinguished Emily from the rest of the ladies, while Joey could be identified as the groom from the multicolor traditional raffia bag that he carried across his shoulder, a nod to his other heritage, the Meta culture in which he was born and bred.

At a traditional Bamileke marriage ceremony, the groom and his family come to receive their wife from the wife givers, the bride's family. Typically, the man would pay a bride price and give gifts of palm wine, palm oil, goats, pigs, chicken, firewood, clothing, jewelry, blankets, electronic items, etc. to the girl's family in order to gain the latter's blessings for a productive and successful married life. The amount of the bride price and gifts vary, but if the bride is a highly educated, successful professional, the groom's bank account would suffer a more severe hit. He would have to spend even more if his lady's family is affluent and have very expensive, fine tastes. Families in some Cameroonian tribes have been known to request even more from the suitor if their daughter is light-skinned or is still a virgin.

Nevertheless, there have been cases where the bride had all these above-mentioned qualities, but the groom did not have to spend anything beyond the basics needed for the celebration, because the girl's family wanted their son-in-law to not have to struggle in the months following the ceremony due to expenses incurred to get married to their daughter.

So was the case of Joey as he did not have to pay a bride price for two reasons. He was marrying a lady from an American family that was not familiar with the financial and material transactions that occurred at traditional Cameroonian marriage ceremonies. Additionally, even if the Goldmans were familiar with that custom, they still would not have taken a dime from their daughter's husband because they were filthy rich, and their immense love, admiration, and regard for him were second only to their daughter's. Emily would not have allowed her parents or anyone to take a penny from her man in exchange for her hand in marriage. She loved Joey to the moon and back, and the first time she and Joey talked about

African wedding practices, she felt that if anything needed to be paid, she should be paying to get married to a uniquely kind, exceptionally caring, and tremendously brilliant man like Joey. She considered herself overwhelmingly blessed to have him in her life, and she never passed on any opportunity to remind him about that.

Thus, the traditional ceremony was mostly the parents of the bride and the groom imparting their blessings and lessons of wisdom to their children. Joey's father told the couple to never allow anything, or anyone come between them and to never allow a dispute, something that they were certain to have from time to time, to linger unresolved beyond bedtime on the date of its occurrence. He proceeded to pour fresh palm wine into a 217-year-old bullhorn cup that had been passed down to the head of the Jumessi family for generations and handed it to his son to drink from it, and then to his daughter-in-law for a sip. It was a symbol of the bestowing of ancestral blessings on the young couple, the future of the family.

The speeches and blessings were followed by what is commonly referred to in Cameroon as Item 11, eating and drinking. The couple was officially married, traditionally, and the ceremony ended around 1:00 am so that everyone could get some rest before the more hectic, Christian American wedding celebration.

With guests from out of state and from Cameroon in town, the lovebirds couldn't depart for their honeymoon immediately after the wedding ceremonies like most couples do. The mothers-in-law spent a considerable amount of time hanging out in the apartment, shopping at Wolfchase and pampering themselves at a spa on Germantown Parkway, while the dads drained several bottles of whiskey while chatting on the balcony every day, for about a week. Anyone that didn't know them could have thought that those two men were very close buddies. Joey was very happy to see his parents get along so well with his in-laws. The latter had come a very long way in four years; from being against their child dating a Black man, to happily blessing her marriage to the same guy and bonding with his parents. Any loving parent would do just that, and even more, for their child.

While the parents were spending quality time together, the bride and the groom took his sister around Shelby County to visit all the places that they had taken his parents to a year earlier and to shop at Wolfchase Galleria. Although the wedding ceremonies were very amazing, the newlyweds and their parents all concurred that the time that they spent bonding together, for a whole week, after the event was more remarkable than anything else.

At the end of that week, the guests, sadly, said goodbye and promised to see one another again very soon. On the same day that they left, Joey and Emily left for Florida to catch a Royal Caribbean cruise ship. Emily wanted them to spend their honeymoon in Kribi, a coastal city that they couldn't visit when they had traveled to Cameroon to see his parents, but Joey suggested that they do something cheaper that they both had never experienced. Sailing on a cruise ship was one of them. Nevertheless, he promised that they would celebrate their 5th anniversary in Kribi.

They had a lot of fun on the cruise ship for seven days, even though they made sure not to stay up too late. Every morning they would go to the gym and workout for an hour. Upon returning, they would shower and order breakfast to the cabin. They would eat slowly on the balcony while reading a newspaper or a magazine to enjoy the view of the ocean and the gentle breeze emanating from it. At around noon, they would get dressed casually and go for a walk around the ship before stopping for lunch and drinks at one of the restaurants on board. They took their time in everything they did, as for the first time in months, they were not thinking about a job, wedding plans, school, and other commitments. Other pastimes that the newlyweds indulged in included go-cart racing, tennis, table tennis, swimming, nightclubbing, and karaoke.

The brief time away from everything, after a very busy few months, was refreshing and invigorating. It only brought them closer to each other and made them more appreciative of their relationship, of their marriage.

When they returned from their getaway, it was time for both of them to return to work. She was going to be starting her 4th week at one of the fastest-growing law firms in Memphis, one led by a friend of her father, while Joey was going into his second year of teaching at Bolton. He had passed the school leadership licensure exam, but he wanted to get at least three years of teaching experience in Tennessee under his belt in order to enhance his chances of landing a job in school administration.

When most couples get married, the next logical step in life is usually purchasing a house and starting a family. Mindful of that, Emily's parents wanted to help them get a place, but Joey, out of pride, said that he would prefer something that he and his wife purchased with their own hard-earned cash. Consequently, in addition to teaching, he coached soccer, tutored candidates for the PRAXIS test, proofread dissertations, edited the books of aspiring authors, and even dabbled in landscaping with a colleague, just to raise enough money for the down payment on a house.

Over 11 months later, he and his wife had more than what they had set as their goal and they started shopping around the county for a place that fit their taste, one that had four bedrooms, a spacious kitchen and living room, an office, a library, a game room, a sunroom, a two-car garage, outside storage built with the same material as the main house, and a spacious yard that was big enough to kick soccer balls in the backyard. They wanted the house to be in a quiet and beautiful neighborhood. Thus, they looked at a few properties in Bartlett, Arlington, Millington, Collierville, and on central Avenue in Memphis, but rejected each of them for missing one or more of their non-negotiables.

Meanwhile, something disgusting to Emily, but amusing to her husband, happened almost every time they took an appointment with a realtor to see a house for sale. They would arrive for the meeting and the realtor, would acknowledge, and speak only to Emily while ignoring the Black man that was with her, like he was not even present, even though they introduced themselves as husband and wife, and the same information was indicated when booking the appointments.

Disgusted by the blatant disregard and disrespect of her husband, Emily would say, "Ask my husband," or "What do you think babe?" whenever the realtor requested input about the type of house they were in the market for, so as to let the bigoted individual know that they were equal partners in the quest for a home.

After two months of persistent searching, they found a three-year old brick house in Germantown that met all of their expectations. They got a good deal on the house, saving almost $30,000 on what they had budgeted, and with the savings, they both agreed that it was time to rid themselves of the old Nissan that Joey had been driving since 2009. It was traded in for a certified preowned Mercedes E450.

Thus, Dr. and Mrs. Jumessi moved into their new home on September 30, 2015, his birthday. They were immensely grateful to God for what they had been able to accomplish together out of tremendous love for each other, in spite of criticism, opposition, and pure hate from some people, including many that they loved dearly. They did not care at all about what anyone said, thought or felt about their relationship, as long as they had each other.

CHAPTER THIRTEEN

DERAILMENT

Anyone who has ever taught a high school class, even for one day, knows that anything could derail even the most effectively planned lesson. It could be something as serious as a security emergency, or minute things like the image or writing on a student's t-shirt, or the arrival of a new student, or the absence of a peer. Great teachers possess the ability to turn such situations into teachable moments and opportunities to unlock student motivation.

One such derailment occurred during 7th period on a Friday in December of 2015. In a comment about the current event assignment, a male student said that he did not know that police brutality could occur in countries that were homogeneously Black until he read an article describing the gruesome use of water cannons, tear gas, batons, bullets, and other violent tactics to quell an uprising in Côte d'Ivoire. The student talked about law enforcement officials in the West African nation torturing those arrested and summarily killing them.

"What surprised me was that these were Black police officers maiming and killing their own kind without remorse and with impunity," he said and then added, "If Black lives matter, why are they doing that?"

In a class taught by a Black immigrant in a classroom filled with brilliant, mostly White, some Black and a couple of Hispanic 17-year-olds, at a time in the United States when news of police violence towards Black citizens was all over the media, that remark was like striking a match near an open can of gasoline.

Some students burst out laughing, while others struggled to find anything funny about what was said.

"What you read about Côte d'Ivoire is not uncommon in dictatorships such as in Congo, Benin, Tchad, Equatorial Guinea, Gabon, Sudan, Togo, Zimbabwe, and Cameroon, where I was born. The leader often uses any means necessary, including violence on their citizens to suppress any opposition to their regime. But you should be extremely careful not to compare what's happening in those countries to what Black people are experiencing here in the United States, because Black lives do matter," Dr. Jumessi responded quickly, with emphasis on his last five words. If he thought that his response had put the matter to rest and he could continue his class, he was wrong, by a very long shot.

"That's just some left-wing hoax that the media is spreading. All lives matter!" retorted Conor, one of the White students who were laughing earlier. The can burst into flames, huge incredibly hot rhetorical flames, that the teacher fought very hard to contain. He knew he could not put out the blaze with threats of punishment as it would have only made things spiral out of control. Instead, he tried to turn it into a somewhat-structured debate, with him as the moderator, allowing everyone to air their opinions without disrespect. He believed that the debate would give him an insight into his students' minds and motivations, and he could use that eventually to plan lessons that were tailored to their interests.

"To say that all lives matter when there is overwhelming evidence of law enforcement killing Black people more than any other racial group of people in America is just simply denying the facts," Jennifer, a usually quiet student, countered, annoyed.

"Which facts? What are the facts?" came a challenge from

William, a peer sitting behind her.

"Well, the evidence is indisputable and overwhelming that our criminal justice system in general is immensely unjust toward Black people. My father and my uncles were just talking about this two days ago. Take the state of Texas for example, according to the *Texas Justice Initiative*, even though Blacks constitute less than 12% of the state's population, they make up 29% of deaths in the custody of police officers, and 27% of the total number civilians who are shot by law enforcement. In another state, statistics released by United State Department of Justice, show that in Ferguson, MO, where Michael Brown was shot by the police, 85% of all vehicle stops between 2012 and 2014, 90% of citations, and 93% of arrest warrants involved Black people, even though they accounted for 67% of the total population of the city. Oh, here's another piece of evidence for you, 'Thomas': research done by renowned anthropologist, Cody T. Ross, found that between 2011 and 2014, there was overwhelming bias in the killing of unarmed Black citizens in the United States compared to the killing of unarmed Whites. Additionally, he found that the probability of being Black, unarmed, and shot by police is about 3.49 times the probability of being White, unarmed, and shot by police on average. Furthermore, and this one is from our great Volunteer State, between 2011 and this year, 2015, Blacks in Nashville were twice as likely to be pulled over by the police and searched and ticketed than Whites. Similar statistics are reported in surveys, studies, reports, and investigations from all over the United States. We could spend a whole day here going over the evidence that law enforcement profiles Blacks and is overwhelmingly more violent towards them than they are toward White Americans, but that would not be enough time to just scratch the surface of this abomination."

"Excellent job looking up and citing evidence, Jennifer. So, William, do you agree that the brutality and injustice toward Black people in America by law enforcement supports the claim that they are acting as if Black lives don't matter?" Dr. Jumessi asked.

"No, because a lot more White people are killed by the police every year, but you don't hear anyone protesting and saying White lives matter."

Another peer, Tamir, quickly rebutted, "You're right that, numerically, more White people are victims of police brutality in the United States, but that's because you, White people, account for about 73% of the total population of this nation. Do you know what percentage of the US population is Black? Approximately 13%, yet, proportionately, we're 3.49 times more likely to be shot by the police. Take this year, 2015, for example; according to the *Washington Post*, the police have shot a total of 990 people this year. Out of that, 494 were White, while 258 were Black, but don't be fooled by these statistics, because, based on the percentage of the total population that's Black, we were three times more likely to be killed by the police in America this year."

"Impressive, Tamir, that's impressive!" Dr. Jumessi complemented. A star football player, Tamir had previously given his teacher and his peers the impression that he ate, drank, and slept only football; nothing else interested him. That was all he wanted to talk about, and his examples in class always had something to do with the sport, but there he was, showing great command of national demographics and evidence-supported speech.

His teacher's praise was gasoline to his rhetorical flame as he added, "The numbers I just gave you do not even include the scores of other Blacks who were killed by the police using other violent means like chokeholds as in the case of Eric Gardner who was killed in New York in 2014."

He went on to cite some examples of the Black victims of police violence that were killed between 2014 and 2015, including Freddie Gray, Michelle Cusseaux, Janisha Fonville, Michael Brown, Walter Scott, William Chapman, Samuel Dubose,

Jamar Clark, and Jeremy Mcdole. The mention of these names did not seem to go well with William who fired back, saying aggressively, "Some of those people you just mentioned had broken the law and were resisting arrest. If they had just complied with the orders of law enforcement officers, at least two of them that I know of for sure, would still be alive today. I'm talking about Eric Gardner and Michael Brown."

William's point got many, including the teacher, disgusted, but, unlike the others, Dr. Jumessi masterfully hid his revulsion at the implication that any unarmed person deserved to be killed if they resisted arrest, or got into an altercation with the police.

"Whether they committed a crime or not, whether they resisted arrest or confronted the police or not, none of these people deserved to be killed. Their lives mattered! I'm happy that the media and activists are raising awareness about the brutality of some police officers, obviously a tiny fraction of them. I just wish that enough light is also shed on the cases of Black immigrants whose lives are ended brutally by police officers. For instance, although the case of Amadou Diallo, an unarmed Guinean immigrant with no criminal record, shot 41 times by four officers in New York City in 1999, garnered significant coverage, the police killing of other Black immigrants over the years has gone almost unnoticed. The case of Ousman Zongo, an unarmed immigrant from Burkina Faso, who in 2003 was also killed by NYPD officers who later found that he had nothing to do with the counterfeiting that he was suspected of, is worth noting. Equally worth mentioning here are the senseless murders of Jonathan Deng, a Sudanese immigrant who was killed by police officers in Iowa City in 2009, Mohamed Bar, a Guinean immigrant who was fatally shot by NYPD officers in 2012, Cameroonian immigrant Charley Keunang, killed by police officers in Los Angeles earlier this year, another Sudanese, Deng Manyoun, whose life was cut short by Louisville, KY cops this year as well as homeless Haitian immigrant, David Felix, slaughtered by NYPD officers this year,

2015. But one of the least known cases is that of Cameroonian Peter Njang, who was killed in 2004 by the police in Silver Springs, MD. He had just arrived in the United States and was living with his uncle. One day, he returned home and realized that he had misplaced his key. So, after knocking on the door in vain, he went to the back of the apartment to see if he could get the attention of someone through the window, but at that time, two passing cops in a cruiser noticed him and took him for a burglar. They told him to come over, and as he was approaching them, he was telling them that he lived in the apartment, that he had misplaced his key and was just trying to see if he could get someone's attention through the window to open the door for him. Unfortunately, as he reached into his pocket to get his ID to prove that he was not telling a lie, that he lived at the address, the officers fatally shot him. Later, they claimed that he had a box cutter, although one was never found, and the officers have never been disciplined. You see, as a result of the fact that most immigrants typically don't have family in this country nor any influential connections in the communities in which they live to raise and sustain the public's attention to the execution of immigrants by police officers, their cases don't get the traction they deserve and are quickly forgotten. So, Conor and William, way too many Black people are killed by the police in the United States, and that is part of the reason why you hear protesters and activists chant loudly that Black lives matter. They're saying that all lives will not matter until Black lives matter, until Blacks are treated with respect by law enforcement and the justice system," Dr. Jumessi said passionately.

Then he added in closing, "The vast majority of cops in this country are incredibly decent, friendly, honorable, and caring men and women, and they are respectful of the value of human life, including that of Black people, and that's something that gives me hope that, progressively, the bad apples would be removed from the system."

As the students were packing their belongings to leave at

the end of class, Antwan, who had not said anything during the passionate debate, stated in reference to Dr. Jumessi's last point that, "It's true that the overwhelming majority of cops are nice, but none of them have a sign on their forehead or on their uniform that identifies them as the good ones. That's why the default position of most Black people in communities around America is to treat all cops with absolute mistrust until they prove themselves to be the trustworthy officers." Many of his peers, including all the Blacks and several White students, agreed with him.

On his way home, Joey thought about the constructive discourse that happened in his last period, and he was happy to have allowed the students to express themselves freely. The discussion had revealed to him that, just because a student never participates in a discussion in class does not mean that he or she is shy or unintelligent. It could just mean that the teacher has not sparked the student's interest enough, or that the instructor has not made his or her lessons relatable to the student. He decided that he would research more innovative ways to connect his lessons to his students' personal experiences and interests in order to enhance their learning and achievement.

While still driving, he called his wife, as usual, to ask about her day and to talk about his. She had been working on the asylum case of a Congolese citizen who had escaped torture and persecution by the government of his home country, but his application for protection from the government of the United States of America had been handicapped by his decision to appear pro se before an immigration judge and his declining of the option to use an interpreter at his merits hearing.

"So, how did the case go, pretty?"

"It was very long and challenging, because of prior errors that had to be corrected, but, in the end, the judge granted him asylum."

"Oh wow! That's amazing, babe. I know his chances of getting reprieve were very slim, given the errors that he made previously; so, you must have made an extremely compelling case in his favor. Congratulations, honey; I'm very proud of you!"

"Thank you, babe; that means a lot to me, coming from you. How was your day?"

He narrated everything about a very smooth Friday, with teaching and learning progressing fluidly until things got off-track during the seventh period when one of his students made a remark about police brutality in Côte d'Ivoire.

"That must have sparked a very heated and, perhaps, confrontational situation in your classroom, didn't it?"

"Yes, it did! It almost spun out of control, but I was able to take control and capitalize on the situation by turning it into a constructive debate about police violence in the United States, and in the process, I learned a lot about my students, such as their rhetorical skills that I did not know they had, what they are passionate about and what motivates them."

He recounted every point made in the debate as much as he could, and then he added, "It was an incredible coincidence to notice that some of the kids who have joked about my accent and have said some stupid, vile, and abhorrent things about Africans, were the same ones denying the existence of bias towards Black people in American law enforcement."

"That's very telling. Good thing you were able to turn this into something constructive and useful."

"Absolutely! I am pleased that I let the situation unfold the way it did. Are you still at work?"

"No, I left as soon as the hearing was over. I'm at home now. How about you, are you almost home?"

"Yes, I'll see you shortly. I love you!"

"OK, babe. I love you more!"

CHAPTER FOURTEEN

A DOVE IN THE TORNADO

The first 10 days in the month of November 2016 saw dramatic events happen in both the United States and Cameroon that changed Joey's life profoundly, forever. On the one hand, the election of a nationalist, xenophobic bigot as president of the United States emboldened white supremacists, Nazis, and nationalists nationwide to come out of the shadows. Acts of hate against Black people and immigrants accelerated, often with the perpetrators expressing pride in their accomplishments and even taunting their victims, their families, and their supporters. In fact, following the election of 2016, hate crimes reached a sixteen-year high nationwide.

On the other hand, peaceful protests that were initiated by the Cameroon Anglophone Civil Society Consortium (CACSC), a group made up of lawyers and teacher trade unions from the English-speaking parts of the country, were met immediately with a massive crack-down by the government. Hundreds of peaceful protesters were tear-gassed, beaten, bruised, and arrested. The unnecessary brutal treatment of individuals who were simply exercising their freedom of expression and assembly, both rights guaranteed by the International Convention on Civil and Political Rights (ICCPR), of which Cameroon is a signatory, only caused the anger and bitterness against the government, which had been boiling for decades, to explode. Things quickly spiraled out of control and plunged the country into a conflict that neither side entertained the appetite to resolve.

Meanwhile, in their August 2019 article captioned *"Trump and Racism: what do the data say?"* Vanessa Williamson and Isabella Gelfand of the Brookings Institution attempted to present the correlation between President Trump's racist rhetoric and racial violence in the United states. They cited data from *"Understanding White Polarization in the 2016 Vote for President: The Sobering Role of Racism and Sexism"*, written by Brian Schafer, Matthew MacWilliams, and Tatisha Nteta and published in *Political Science Quarterly*, volume 123 in November of 2018, to enhance their claim that the support of Mr. Trump was spurred by racism and xenophobia. The dramatic spike in hate crimes in counties where Trump campaigned and won by huge margins in 2016 "... was the second largest uptick in hate crimes in the 25 years for which data are available, second only to the spike after September 11, 2001," according to these researchers.

Another example they gave to support their claim was a 2017 study in which "... researchers randomly exposed respondents to racist comments made by the President." When exposed to racist statements the president had made about minorities such as "When Mexico sends its people, they're not sending their best. They're sending people that have lots of problems... They're bringing drugs. They're bringing crime. They're rapists..." the respondents "...were more likely to write derogatory things, not only about Mexican people, but also about other groups as well," including Blacks, and immigrants from other countries. Therefore, the President's statement in August 2017 that there were "fine people on both sides" after clashes between neo-Nazi white supremacists and anti-hate protesters in Charlottesville, VA couldn't have been racial-harmony-fostering.

Similarly, his reference to Black African nations and Haiti as "shithole countries" was just as racist as when he told a group of United State Congress women of color to "go back" and fix the "crime-infested places" they originally came from.

And these comments, along with hundreds of others that he made since becoming president in 2016, and even while he was on the presidential campaign trail, fanned the flames of racial tensions and caused vicious attacks against immigrants to rise exponentially, from microaggressions to violent attacks that resulted in loss of life and damage to property.

The rapid acceleration of public manifestations of hate against minority groups, especially Blacks, deeply troubled Joey and caused him to start fearing for his own life. He was traumatized by the savage killing of Ahmaud Aubery on February 23rd, 2020. The fact that three White men could pursue an unarmed 25-year-old, who was jogging down the street, and shoot him to death, in broad daylight, gave him goosebumps. Even more agonizing to him was the fact that the murderers walked around freely for three months before the public's outcry, protests, and pressure led to their arrest.

After Ahmaud Aubery's murder, Joey would not get out of the house unnecessarily, and he would take identification documents, including his Tennessee driver's license and his certificate of naturalization whenever he did, even when he left his home for simple things like going to the mailbox in front of his house, going for a jog down the street, or walking to the park. He did not want to be stopped by the police anywhere without proper identification as that could lead to some dangerous consequences, based on what was happening to Black people just about everywhere in America.

His worst fear materialized on the night of June 3rd, 2020 as he was returning home from participating in a *Black Lives Matter* protest following the heinous, repulsive, and revolting killing of George Floyd by Minneapolis, MN police officers on May 25th of the same year. He was turning on Dogwood Road to get into his neighborhood around 10:00 pm when a black, unmarked Chevy Tahoe that had been trailing him for about 3 minutes, suddenly had blue lights flashing all over its windshield. Knowing exactly what that meant, he quickly recalled the advice that an old colleague had given him when he had started driving in Indianola over 10 years earlier. Thus, he found an area that was well-lit and pulled over on the side of the road as the SUV eased to a stop a few feet behind him. A 6-foot-tall, bald police officer with a thick gray mustache and muscles that stretched his black, short-sleeve polo shirt almost to a breaking point alighted from the Tahoe. The White cop, probably in his fifties, walked towards the black Mercedes sedan that had parked directly under a streetlight.

Joey had been pulled over by the police twice in the 11 years that he had lived in the United States. The first time was for speeding when he was late for class at Delta State University. Back then, he admitted his fault and was issued a speeding ticket. The second time was on I-55, still in Mississippi. He and his wife were returning to Memphis from Jackson, Mississippi one night when he got pulled over by the Highway Patrol. The officer looked at his license and registration with the help of a flashlight, then he flashed the light in the driver's face and back on the driver's license. He repeated these steps again thrice without telling him why he was stopped. Then, still quiet, the officer went on the passenger side, and without the flashlight in Emily's face, he asked, "Ma'am, are you OK?"

"Yes, officer," she responded. "May we know why you pulled us over?" she asked.

Ignoring her question, the patrolman returned Joey's license and registration and said, "Y'all have a good night."

Joey drove off, wondering what the reason for the stop was. His wife as irate, not just because of what the officer had done to them, but also because she did not get a good look at the officer's name on his uniform to report him the next day.

But, unlike the previous times that Joey was pulled over, something about the third time, on Dogwood Road, got him incredibly nervous, although he could not tell exactly what that was. Maybe it was just the political and social climate in the country, especially during the last days of May and the start of June. His window was rolled all the way down and both of his hands were on the steering wheel, exactly as strongly advised by his friend a decade earlier.

"Is this your car?" the bulky officer asked, without greeting.

"Yes, sir!" Joey answered nervously.

"License and registration please."

"May I have permission to reach for my wallet in my pocket to get my license?"

"Yes, go ahead" the cop said, while keeping his right hand on his gun. "What are you doing in this neighborhood by the way?" he asked while the driver was struggling to pull his license out of his wallet, his hands trembling.

"I live right down the street," responded Joey while handing the policeman the documents he requested.

The cop retreated to his SUV for a few minutes before returning and handing the documents to Joey who had his hands firmly on the wheel while sitting up straight and avoiding any sudden moves. Without explaining why he was pulled over or anything, the officer gave back the documents and said, "Goodnight!"

"But you didn't tell me..." he was about to ask the rude and prejudicial officer why he had been pulled over, but he suddenly heard his mother's gentle voice imploring him to let it go, not to become a statistic.

"What did you say?" the cop asked.

"Never mind. Thank you, sir. Good night!" Joey responded.

Joey spent three minutes on the side of the road after he was allowed to go, trying to put himself back together. That's when he noticed that his jeans were a little wet near the groin area. Seething and frustrated by what he and millions of other Black people were enduring on a daily basis in the United States, he drove home. Upon arriving at his residence, he went and took a shower and put on fresh clothes. Then, he sat his pregnant wife on the living room couch and told her about the loathsome police stop. He cautioned her to not worry about it because, in her state, any stress could have adverse consequences on the pregnancy.

"How can I take it easy when my husband is harassed by a police officer on the side of the road in the middle of the night just because of the color of his skin? A Black man driving a luxury car in an upscale neighborhood is all of a sudden suspicious activity? I'm sick and tired of this nonsense!" she exclaimed.

It was clear that she was not just worried about her husband. She was fretful about the America that her Black son would be arriving into at any moment. She did not know that was the same reason that caused her husband to join the protesters downtown Memphis earlier that day. He did his best to calm her down.

"I need you not to stress yourself up about this, honey. God is in control; he's going to protect us as he has been doing; everything will be alright," he comforted her, as she sunk her head into his chest, sobbing.

He continued to whisper soothing, reassuring words while gently rubbing her back until all the tension eased out of her body, and they eventually went to bed.

When he lay down that night, he tried to go to sleep, but he could not, as not only were the racial tensions and the devastation caused by COVID-19, especially in minority groups in the United States, weighing heavily on his mind, but also, the grim tidings from his home country, Cameroon, troubled him gravely.

The brutal use of force in dictatorships to quell a protest or squash an uprising of the citizens often works to stop the physical manifestations; that's why it's the main strategy, or, perhaps, the only one that autocrats deploy to suppress civil disobedience. However, while this method may force the protesters to retreat, to get out of the streets, it doesn't kill the sentiments, the grievances that led to the uprising in the first place, nor does it silence the disaffected people. The anger would just keep growing until the point where the citizens would be fed up and would be willing to lose their lives in the fight for change, telling the government, unequivocally, "Give us a better life or give us death!"

That is precisely what happened with the ongoing tension in Joey's home country. When the lawyers and teachers took to the streets in Limbe, Bamenda, Buea, and other cities in Anglophone Cameroon in November 2016 to tell the government, for the millionth time, to stop assimilating and infiltrating the common law system that was in effect in the English-speaking regions, they were met with vicious, virulent violence. The citizens' pursuit of a fair and effective judicial system was not something that the government was willing to allow.

Additionally, the disgruntled legal and education professionals wanted all the laws that were written exclusively in French to be translated into the second official language, English and for English-speaking or effectively bilingual judges to be appointed for all the courtrooms in Anglophone Cameroon.

Similarly, the protesters demanded that the common law system of education be implemented and strengthened in the Anglo-Saxon universities of Bamenda and Buea, possibly with the opening of a law school. The latter would train legal minds that would be tailored to effectively address the needs of Anglophone Cameroonians.

In typical fashion, the government unleashed thousands of heavily armed soldiers and police officers on the hundreds of peacefully protesting attorneys and educators, expecting that batons and bullets would achieve the results that the autocratic regime had gotten used to during its 34-year reign. The use of force was a colossal mistake, as the brutality of the law enforcement officers simply poured gasoline into the fire, causing it to spread wildly and quickly.

By December 2016, the peaceful protest initiated by lawyers and teachers had transformed into a popular demand for the secession of Anglophone Cameroon, also called Southern Cameroons, from the Republic of Cameroon, a demand that only made the government flood cities, towns, and villages in the two regions with all its military might. Such a move only radicalized the rebelling citizens, forcing them to arm and defend themselves by any means necessary. Consequently, the conflict got extremely bloody as it stubbornly raged on, thus surprising the government every step of the way.

Therefore, what the lady from whom Joey had bought mangoes at Mbon Market during his visit to Cameroon in May 2012 had predicted was actually happening, and he was very worried about the safety of his family, although, as usual, his parents told him that they were as safe in Mbengwi as the natives, because the city was their adopted home for more than 40 years. They were right, as they were not bothered by anyone, even as the struggle metastasized.

Two years later, by the close of 2018, the incredibly violent war for the independence of Southern Cameroons, to create a better country called Ambazonia, had led to the killing of at least 4000 civilians in the disgruntled regions. In addition to the fatalities, by the second anniversary of the conflict, more than 63,000 citizens had fled to neighboring Nigeria, while close to a million more had sought refuge in other cities in Francophone Cameroon.

The rapidly and endlessly spreading conflict attracted the attention of world leaders and influential organization, but instead of heeding the pleas from the United States, Britain, France, Switzerland, Germany, and many other nations, and from international organizations like the United Nations, the African Union, and the European Union, for a negotiated resolution without preconditions, the government simply doubled down. It arrested, jailed, and killed more rebels, including the leaders of the separatist movement. The destruction of property, loss of lives on both sides worsened the hardship of the citizens of Anglophone Cameroon and inflicted immense damage to the national economy. Thus, the pangs of the war that started in two provinces was being experienced by everyone nationwide.

The crisis got so dire that the government was compelled to accept the international community's call for dialogue with the opposition factions in September of 2019. However, the five-day talks, from September 30th to October 4th, achieved nothing significant, because they were not convened in good faith, without preconditions as advised. For instance, regarding the key issue of the independence of the English-speaking regions, the government said before the meeting that it was never going to allow a separation of any of its ten regions. Nevertheless, it agreed during the negotiations to grant the Anglophone regions special status that would allow them some autonomy in decision making and management of their affairs.

That concession was not what the rebels wanted. As a result, the war raged on throughout the rest of that year and into 2020, to the chagrin of exhausted, frustrated, and despairing citizens, who did not just have to endure the pains of the war but were also left helpless and vulnerable in the face of the rapidly spreading and very deadly COVID-19 pandemic.

Thus, the thoughts about things that were happening in both of his homes, Cameroon and the United States, troubled Joey tremendously, depriving him of sleep as he lay in bed that night of June 3rd, 2020, even though he had a couple of things going on in his life that the average person would be ecstatic about and would not have any trouble sleeping. For example, after trying unsuccessfully to have a baby for six years, his wife was pregnant and was going to deliver their first child at any moment. Additionally, since he graduated with a doctorate in educational leadership, he had not been successful in getting a job in that area, but on May 31st, 2020, he was hired as an instructional advisor by his school district because of his exceptional performance in the classroom.

How could a mind that was anxious find peace? Such was his predicament that night as he lay fully awake next to his sleeping wife all night. What could he do to end racism and xenophobia in the United States? What could he do to eradicate the corruption and end the marginalization of Anglophones that had led to a brutal war that had brought his country of birth to its knees? Could he just ignore these issues and live his life selfishly like many people were doing, minding just their own affairs and not caring about what was happening to others? His life was great. He had what most people anywhere in the world would call a successful life, with a good job, a mansion, luxury cars, an amazing wife, a son on the way, a supportive family back home in Cameroon, exceptional in-laws, and good health. He had achieved the American dream and ought to be sleeping like a sloth.

As he pondered these issues, the weight of which were sinking his mind like the weight of two elephants, he realized that they could only be solved if everyone, including himself, became less selfish and started working for the good of their community, their country. People had to start practicing the type of positive, productive change that they wanted to see happen in their home, community, and country. The United States as he knew it was too toxic for minorities. Conditions in Cameroon were unbearable for most citizens, especially those in the Anglophone regions. Neither the United States nor Cameroon was a country that he wished for his son to be born or to grow up in. He had to do something to help make things better, in order not to look embarrassed and stupid if things got worse and his son asked him one day, "Daddy, what was your contribution to the fight to end racism and xenophobia in the United States and the suffering of the people in Cameroon?"

He gave up trying to go to sleep at 7:00 am and went into

the kitchen to prepare breakfast for Emily. He served her a meal in bed consisting of an omelet, bacon, French toast, chopped assorted fruits and coffee. He made sure that she didn't need anything before he went and sat in the stressless recliner in the sunroom to drink his coffee. As he sat there, his mind kept bring up the questions that had kept him up all night.

By 10:00 am he had come up with a list of things he believed he could do. Firstly, he thought that, in addition to participating in protests and stirring up what the great congressman, John Lewis, called good trouble, he would also make significant donations regularly to genuine organizations that were engaged in active, verifiable fight for social justice in the United States and in Cameroon.

Furthermore, he concluded that it was time to do something that he first thought about during his visit to Cameroon in 2012: publish a book or at least, an article about the plight of the Anglophone citizens and about the systemic corruption in Cameroon. The more people wrote about the issues, the more awareness would be spread to different parts of the globe, and widespread awareness about a problem has been known to be crucial in the pursuit of a meaningful solution. He understood that the things he was opting to do would expose him to danger, especially in Cameroon where the autocratic government was famous for employing extreme violence to silence its critics, but he believed the risk of standing on the sideline far outweighed that of becoming actively involved in the fight for social justice and prosperity for all in Cameroon and in the United States.

Feeling better after coming up with those concrete, attainable steps, he went back to bed to give sleep another shot. It was already noon, and before long he was fast asleep. At some point in that deep slumber, he had a dream in which he had his teenage son and his wife in a white Cadillac Escalade, and they were driving through Harrison, AR one evening when they had a flat tire. He got out the SUV to replace the tire, but as soon as he pulled out the spare one, he noticed that it was totally deflated. They were stuck on the side of a road on both sides of which was just a sea of corn growing. He called Allstate roadside assistance and he was told that help was on the way, but that the person could not get to them until after an hour.

As he and his family sat there waiting patiently, an old white pickup truck that looked like a 1960 Ford F-100 appeared from the opposite direction. There were three men in the cabin while three others were standing on the bed. The three behind were each flying a large flag. One of them was carrying a huge American flag while another held a blue, white, and red Trump banner. The words on the latter were not fully visible as it was getting dark, and the flag was waving in the steady wind, but one of them was "Again." The third person, sandwiched between the other two, was proudly waving a confederate flag that was the size of the first two combined.

The pickup truck came to a stop across the road from the white SUV and the six individuals in it, all dressed in white robes and hoods that had two holes on the face, jumped out and rushed towards the stranded family.

Quickly surrounded by the unmistakable members of the Ku Klux Klan, Joey thought about reaching for the pistol that he always carried in his glove compartment whenever he was driving his family out of town, but before he could do that, a voice behind one of the scary masks said, "Don't be afraid my brother! We're not going to harm you and your family. We just saw that your truck had broken down, and we decided to stop and see if we could help. So how can we help you guys get back on the road?"

Everyone in the SUV was shocked by what they had just heard. Members of the KKK, in the most racist town in America, rushing to the aid of a biracial family. Unbelievable!

Joey explained to them what had happened and what he needed. One of the men returned to the truck and came back with an electric pump.

"Here, stick this in your cigarette lighter while I pump some air in your spare tire, and you guys will be on your way shortly!"

The men, without taking their masks off at any moment, replaced the flat tire with the inflated spare, packed up the tools and placed them neatly in the rear of the SUV and wished the rescued family a safe trip back to Germantown, TN. Each of them exchanged contact information with Joey and expressed the desire to get together for drinks and BBQ one day soon in Memphis.

Moments later, as they got back on the road, Joey called his best friend, John, to tell him the shocking thing that had just happened to him and his family, but instead of being surprised, John said that the encounter was not an outlier. He said that racism was fading away rapidly around the United States. He also added that he was finalizing plans to move his entire family to Cameroon in three weeks.

"Bro, isn't that a very dangerous thing to do? Are you not worried about your safety? How are you going to provide for Jessica and the kids in a country that is in a civil war and is experiencing a severe economic crisis?"

"This man, have you been living under a rock or something? Don't you know that the war ended two years ago and there is a new president, an Anglophone, now in Cameroon? In a very short time, the man has transformed the country into one of the most prosperous on the continent, and most Cameroonians in the diaspora are going back home to take advantage of the tremendous opportunities that have been created. I'm tired of the stressful life of working just to pay bills in America. I'm going home to participate in rebuilding my homeland!"

"You're right; I must have been living under a rock, because I had no idea about any of these things. What's the name of the...?" He was going to find out more about the changes he did not know had happened in Cameroon when an adorable voice that he loved dearly interrupted.

"Babe!" Emily called as she gently shook him. "Honey, wake up! We have to go! I think the baby is coming!"

That was enough to get even a sedated sloth sprinting into action. He jumped out of bed, put on the first clothes that he saw, gathered all the baby items that they had prepared for that moment and threw them in the trunk. Then he returned to the house and carried his wife to the car. He sat her in the back of the Mercedes because she was in so much pain and needed to be able to lie down or lean if she needed to.

He sped down the street as fast as he could until they made it to the hospital in Bartlett. They arrived just in time, as within a few minutes, Joey Jumessi III was born, two weeks before his original due date. His father had awakened from a dream in which he was in a better place to rush his wife to the hospital to welcome their long-awaited son into a different world, one that was plagued by social injustice, racism, xenophobia, tribalism, corruption, discrimination, and to make matters worse, a very deadly and highly infectious COVID-19 pandemic. However, his parents had hope that the future would be brighter, both for the United States and Cameroon. They were hopeful that baby Joey would grow up in a country where he would be judged by the content of his character, not by the color of his skin, and he would be able to go wherever he wanted, whenever he wanted, and be whatever he aspired to be without fear of becoming a statistic of hate and discrimination. They were hopeful that they would one day take their son to visit his grandparents in the peaceful and prosperous Cameroon that John described in the dream.

ABOUT ATMOSPHERE PRESS

Atmosphere Press is an independent, full-service publish-er for excellent books in all genres and for all audiences. Learn more about what we do at atmospherepress.com.

We encourage you to check out some of Atmosphere's latest releases, which are available at Amazon.com and via order from your local bookstore:

Twisted Silver Spoons, a novel by Karen M. Wicks

Queen of Crows, a novel by S.L. Wilton

The Summer Festival is Murder, a novel by Jill M. Lyon

The Past We Step Into, stories by Richard Scharine

Swimming with the Angels, a novel by Colin Kersey

Island of Dead Gods, a novel by Verena Mahlow

Cloakers, a novel by Alexandra Lapointe

Twins Daze, a novel by Jerry Petersen

Embargo on Hope, a novel by Justin Doyle

Abaddon Illusion, a novel by Lindsey Bakken

Blackland: A Utopian Novel, by Richard A. Jones

The Jesus Nut, a novel by John Prather

The Embers of Tradition, a novel by Chukwudum Okeke

Saints and Martyrs: A Novel, by Aaron Roe

When I Am Ashes, a novel by Amber Rose

ABOUT THE AUTHOR

Antoine F. Gnintedem is a renowned educator both in the United States and across the world. As a linguistic consultant, he has worked for the Department of Defense, the Department of Justice, and the Department of Homeland Security. In addition, he has served as an educational assessment expert for leading national and international testing companies. His academic achievements include a PhD in English language and literature and another doctorate in educational leadership. As a member of the Rotary Club of Memphis, he derives tremendous satisfaction from doing community service in and around Shelby County, TN. Dr. Gnintedem is also the author of *Doom, Gloom, and the Pursuit of the Sun,* a work of historical fiction that has received outstanding reviews around the world.

CPSIA information can be obtained
at www.ICGtesting.com
Printed in the USA
LVHW090000210222
711587LV00001B/1/J